Second Edition

VISUAL TENNIS

JOHN YANDELL

Human Kinetics

Library of Congress Cataloging-in-Publication Data

Yandell, John.
    Visual tennis / John Yandell. -- 2nd ed.
       p.   cm.
    Includes bibliographical references (p.).
    ISBN 0-88011-803-2
    1. Tennis--Psychological aspects.   2. Imagery (Psychology)
    3. Visualization.   I. Title.
    GV1002.9.P75Y356   1998
    796.342'01--dc21

            98-28997
            CIP

ISBN: 0-88011-803-2

Copyright © 1990, 1999 by John Yandell

Acquisitions Editor: Martin Barnard; **Developmental Editor:** C.E. Petit, JD; **Assistant Editor:** Cassandra Mitchell; **Copyeditor:** Bob Replinger; **Proofreader:** Ann Bruehler; **Graphic Designer:** Nancy Rasmus; **Graphic Artists:** Angela Snyder and Tara Welsch; **Photo Editor:** Boyd LaFoon; **Cover Designer:** Jack Davis; **Photographer (cover):** Clive Brunskill/Allsport; **Photographer (interior):** Julie Polunsky, except where noted; **Printer:** United Graphics

Human Kinetics books are available at special discounts for bulk purchase. Special editions or book excerpts can also be created to specification. For details, contact the Special Sales Manager at Human Kinetics.

Printed in the United States of America   10 9 8 7 6 5 4 3 2 1

Human Kinetics
Web site: http://www.humankinetics.com/

United States: Human Kinetics, P.O. Box 5076, Champaign, IL 61825-5076
1-800-747-4457
e-mail: humank@hkusa.com

Canada: Human Kinetics, 475 Devonshire Road Unit 100, Windsor, ON N8Y 2L5
1-800-465-7301 (in Canada only)
e-mail: humank@hkcanada.com

Europe: Human Kinetics, P.O. Box IW14, Leeds LS16 6TR, United Kingdom
(44) 1132 781708
e-mail: humank@hkeurope.com

Australia: Human Kinetics, 57A Price Avenue, Lower Mitcham, South Australia 5062
(088) 277 1555
e-mail: humank@hkaustralia.com

New Zealand: Human Kinetics, P.O. Box 105-231, Auckland 1
(09) 523 3462
e-mail: humank@hknewz.com

CONTENTS

Foreword iv

Preface v

Acknowledgments ix

Chapter 1   Visualizing Your Technique **1**

Chapter 2   Modeling the Classical Style **17**

Chapter 3   Visual Tennis Grips **27**

Chapter 4   The Forehand **33**

Chapter 5   The Backhand **53**

Chapter 6   Playing the Net **85**

Chapter 7   The Serve **127**

Chapter 8   Court Movement **153**

Chapter 9   Progressive Stroke Development **165**

References 179

About the Author 181

FOREWORD

Visual Tennis is a very effective way for people to learn or improve their tennis. I can say that from personal experience.

At a time when I needed to work on my serve, I was able to recover its effectiveness through the work I did with John.

Tennis tips are worth about a dime a dozen. It seems every coach has a different theory about every stroke.

I decided to use John's technique because I liked the idea of approaching the problem visually. When we viewed my serve on video, the problem was obvious, and so was the solution.

By focusing on an image of my backswing from the instructional video John and I had made, I eliminated the problem and recovered the original shape of the motion.

I like to keep things simple. It doesn't work to think too much on the tennis court. John's approach using images made a difference for me. My advice is to try it yourself and see if you have the same result.

John McEnroe

PREFACE

"OK, I want you to prepare early, swing low to high, keep a firm wrist, rotate your hips, make contact in front, bend your knees, and keep your eye on the ball. And remember to stay relaxed!"

Does this sound like your last tennis lesson? You hit one ball and your teaching pro says, "OK, not bad!" Then the flow of technical information starts again. "Racket back, step into the shot, and remember to follow through!" And that's just for your forehand. Perhaps you've taken lessons like this. You think you know exactly what you need to work on, but you are frustrated because you cannot apply the information to make real progress in your level of play.

Compare this traditional lesson situation to another experience that most players have had. You watched great tennis on television, at a tournament, or in a match between players you admire at your club or public courts. You studied the shot-making and were caught up in the drama of the exchanges. You felt as if you were playing the match yourself. The next time you went to the courts, it was as if you had absorbed something directly from the other players. Your tennis felt effortless, and you made every shot you tried. The experience was exhilarating. You had no idea you could play so well or enjoy the game so completely.

In lessons, hours of diligent work often leave you frustrated with your lack of improvement. But simply watching great tennis can raise your level of play without apparent effort! How can this be? The frustration many players experience in traditional tennis lessons stems from the way lessons deliver information, primarily through detailed verbal descriptions of technique. This is not the way most players learn. The preference of most learners is for precise visual demonstrations, the opportunity to involve the body directly in learning, and, especially, the opportunity to evaluate the learning process by references to clear models. A survey of learning style preferences conducted by Dr. Gary Price (1996), a researcher at the University of Kansas, showed that less than 20 percent of people prefer auditory input as the primary information source in the learning environment. Most learners prefer input that is primarily visual, kinesthetic, and tactile.

This research in learning theory is supported by numerous anecdotes about how top players developed their games—by watching and imitating other top players. For most elite players, learning to play great tennis isn't a matter of analyzing and listening. It's a matter of *seeing and feeling*. Watching great tennis works in the same way, which explains why the experience causes so many players to play better on a spontaneous basis. Visual Tennis was designed to give you, in a systematic way, the benefits of direct, nonverbal input. Using the system, you will learn to create routinely the kind of peak performance that most players experience only occasionally.

Visual Tennis works by teaching you to process information in a new way, through *visualization.* As noted sport psychologist Jim Loehr (1986) defines it, "Visualization is thinking in pictures." Visual Tennis teaches you how to think about tennis in pictures rather than words. The pictures you will learn through the system have both a visual and a kinesthetic component. They help you imagine what good technique looks like and how it feels. Visual Tennis is a teaching technology that works with your body's natural learning process to provide the direct visual and physical input you need to develop or improve any stroke, the way great players learn instinctively. If you have struggled in traditional lessons and felt bombarded by technical information, Visual Tennis offers the opportunity to try a different approach—an approach that may allow you to discover, for the first time, your real potential as a player.

The Visual Tennis training program has three interrelated components:

- First, it teaches you to develop classical stroke patterns of extremely high technical quality. The heart of the system is the creation of a series of physical and mental models for classical stroke patterns. The model images and the teaching progressions teach the stroke patterns from the ground up. They also allow you to identify and eliminate specific problems or develop advanced elements of technique, for example, using the legs and the shoulders on the serve the way the top pros do.

- The second training component shows you how to use your model images as a bridge from the physical game to the mental game. Mastering the stroke imagery allows you to develop the physical and mental games simultaneously, as two halves of the same whole. By learning to visualize key stroke images systematically in actual play, you can develop the ability to hit your best shots under competitive pressure. This process parallels the reports of top players, who often spontaneously visualize shots before hitting them.

- The third training component provides a series of offcourt visualization training exercises that use imagery to strengthen both the development of the basic stroke patterns and your ability to use them on court under pressure. Research has established that offcourt mental rehearsal is a powerful factor in accelerating learning and competitive performance. The Visual Tennis system shows you how to integrate its benefits into your tennis.

In recent years tennis coaching has made significant advances in areas such as cross-training, mental-toughness training, and statistical analysis of matches. But if you observe players below the highest competitive levels, you know that many matches are decided by unforced errors stemming from poor technique or the inability to make easy shots under pressure. The Visual Tennis system brings the most basic aspect of the game—hitting the strokes—to the same level of sophistication and effectiveness.

At our tennis school, clinics, and camps in northern California and around the country, we have proven the effectiveness of the approach across a wide range of tennis ages and abilities—beginning children and beginning adults, recreational and club players at all levels, championship USTA league and high school teams, highly ranked junior players, ranked adult NTRP and senior tournament players, college players, and players from all levels of professional tennis, including Grand Slam champions Gabriella Sabatini and John McEnroe. One student described it this way: "Visual Tennis allowed me to achieve a consistency and ability to reproduce my strokes in matches that elevated my game to an entirely new level."

I know from speaking and corresponding with players and coaches around the world how many tennis players have had the same success using the Visual Tennis system. Now you have the same opportunity. We want to hear about your experience using Visual Tennis. Please write us at this address:

John Yandell Tennis School
828 Franklin Street Suite 204
San Francisco, California 94102
videoten@ isp.net

ACKNOWLEDGMENTS

Visual Tennis is the outcome of a 30-year quest to understand how to play tennis and how to teach it to others. Along the way I have been influenced by many coaches, teachers, and players. The list begins with my first coach, Frank Ward, who taught me to be a competitor and later a teacher and coach, and Bill Austin, who taught me to hit a backhand with a single image.

Alan Davis took a chance and gave me the head pro job at Golden Gate Park. Scott Murphy, Charlie Hoeveler, and Weston Reese, have each read parts of this work at various stages. Watching my friend Peter Pearson was the source of many of the early spontaneous visual learning experiences that spurred the development of this system.

Dick Gould, legendary coach at Stanford University, first introduced me to stroke checkpoints and muscle-memory corrections, both of which are core aspects of the Visual Tennis approach. The chapter on court movement is drawn largely from principles I learned in my work with University of California at Santa Cruz coach Bob Hansen. The written work of Jim Loehr and Allen Fox sets the standard for tennis instruction. Their encouragement has been a source of inspiration and confidence.

Special recognition goes to the players and teachers who have worked with me over the years in developing and teaching Visual Tennis: Mike Friedman, Julie Montague, Rob Kelton, Clif West, Greg Swendsen, Jay Ginwale, Matt Gould, Derek Williams, Sara Welch, Natalie Delagnes, Claudine Delagnes, Betina Suessman, Jessica Sloan, Graeme Boushey, Alexandra Delanghe, Megan McEwen, Lydia Stone, and Michelle Parenti, to name a few.

What can I say that hasn't already been said about John McEnroe? I have been fortunate to share the unique benefit of his input, enthusiasm, and support. Sadie Carlson has worked with me not only as a player and teacher but also in demonstrating the models for this second edition. In addition to demonstrating the models, Kerry Mitchell, head pro at John Yandell Tennis School, has helped the system evolve through both his teaching and his contributions to the second edition.

Devin Sconyers, Director of Tennis at the San Francisco Tennis Club, made his facility available for the photo sequences. Julie Polunsky, Michael Isabell, and Perry Joiner did a fabulous job of capturing the models on film. Special thanks go to Steve Dunn from Wilson Sporting Goods, and Roland Seydel and Martin Mulligan from Fila. I want to recognize the editing team at Human Kinetics: Martin Barnard for seeing the potential in a revised edition, and Charlie Petit and Cassandra Mitchell for sculpting it into the form you see here. Finally, to my wife, Isabel Santis: thanks for your insight, humor, and for sharing so many wonderful things besides tennis.

CHAPTER 1

VISUALIZING YOUR TECHNIQUE

Most tennis players have had the experience of playing at a new level after watching great tennis. It happened to me for the first time at age 12 after watching Rod Laver and Ken Rosewall on television. I played afterward with my brother on our neighborhood courts and still remember the elation of hitting new shots.

Many great players recall that they learned how to play simply by watching others. John McEnroe put it this way: "When I was learning to play, I just watched Rod Laver and tried to do what he did." Ivan Lendl told me that as a junior he would play much better after ball-boying matches for the top Czechoslovakian players: "Being on the court so close to the players I saw things, and then I would start to do them myself," he said.

Billie Jean King studied the first serve-and-volley player in women's tennis, Alice Marble, and copied her service motion. American Todd Martin, a world top-10 player, modeled his two-handed backhand on Jimmy Connors and improved his serve by studying pictures of the motion Boris Becker used in his first Wimbledon win. As Martin explains, "Every aspiring athlete should look and see how certain players do things, and then put his own twist on it. It's how we learn."

It is well known that as a junior player, Pete Sampras switched from a two-handed to a one-handed backhand, starting with a grip that Don Budge, the first Grand Slam champion, demonstrated personally to Sampras's coach, Pete Fischer. When Sampras was 12, Fischer showed him 16-millimeter black-and-white films of Rod Laver playing at his peak in the 1960s. Together they developed Pete's game based on the Australian attacking style, which they believed was the key to winning Wimbledon. "I always had an image in the mind of what a tennis player should look like," Fischer has said. "When I took Pete on as a student, I just felt I had an unlimited amount of time to make Pete into that image."

You can see this modeling, or direct learning, in the history of junior tennis. The success of Jimmy Connors and Chris Evert was directly responsible for the acceptance and eventual dominance of the two-handed backhand, a stroke that previously almost no coach or teaching pro would teach. Bjorn Borg started the movement to western grips and heavy topspin—despite universal criticism of his strokes from the tennis establishment. Almost everyone who has observed junior tennis can remember seeing junior players whose strokes and mannerisms, not to mention hairstyle and clothing, mirrored a particular top pro. Most of these young players learned their stroke patterns by watching the top players, usually on television, and modeling their games after those images.

Top players are often puzzled or annoyed when tennis writers or teaching pros ask them detailed technical questions. Pete Sampras said, "I can't really describe to you how I hit my forehand—it's just a natural feeling." For top players the learning process seems to occur at a deeper subverbal level. A teaching pro who had a chance meeting with a top pro player in an airport asked if the pro could show him how he hit his famous two-handed backhand. "Like this," the pro replied. Without a racket, he began to model his distinctive two-handed motion. The teaching pro began to ask the player technical questions about his shoulder and arm positions, but the player cut him off. "I don't know about that stuff, man! I just do this," he said and went back to modeling his stroke.

Great players may have the natural ability to develop their games simply by observing and modeling themselves after other great players. As former world-class player and television commentator Barry McKay put it, "A good athlete can instantly copy a swing pattern." But most recreational and competitive players need more help. The Visual Tennis system provides you a method to learn to do what the top players do instinctively.

Put simply, the system teaches you to think about tennis in pictures. It does this by abstracting the key elements of classical technique into simple physical models and mental images, and then infuses them directly into your nervous system. Sport psychologist Rainer Martens (1992) has written that "Both experimental and scientific evidence demonstrate the power of imagery in helping athletes develop physical and psychological skills." Visual Tennis is the first teaching system based on the systematic use of imagery. It overcomes the limitations of traditional lessons that rely primarily on verbal explanations and tips. Instead it communicates directly with your body in the visual and kinesthetic learning style that, research shows, most people prefer.

Using the system, many players have learned to transcend the perceived limitations of their games. A 40-year-old club player described it this way:

> I had played tennis most of my life and had reached a plateau that I inwardly believed to be the limit of my natural ability. To my surprise, as I began to work in the system, I noticed real and fundamental improvements. With that came a whole newfound enjoyment of tennis. I found people complimenting my game, and I started playing and competing with a far more widespread group than I could ever have before. The whole experience has enabled me to discover new dimensions in the game and in my ongoing possibilities for improvement, not to mention the enjoyment in playing the best tennis of my life.

DEVELOPING STROKE PATTERNS

The first component in the Visual Tennis system is the construction or correction of basic stroke patterns. The system teaches classical tennis by showing you how to create a physical model of the stroke and, at the same time, an internal mental model. This mental picture is a kinesthetic image, an image that includes a feeling component. When you visualize what a stroke looks like, you also visualize how it feels. A career educator who trained at our tennis school described the process in one sentence: "The visual image that you see translates into a motor image that you feel."

Compared with traditional instruction, the models reduce the amount of information you must absorb and make it more specific. For a given stroke you learn to visualize a technical image of the pattern and, at the same time, learn to swing the racket according to the image. The role of the visual model is critical. If you cannot see yourself swing the racket correctly in your mind, you will be unable to swing it correctly on the court. Learning a clear mental model

© Gus Bower

The classical two-handed backhand, as shown by Martina Hingis. Note that her wrist has not released during contact, but has remained laid back with the elbow bent. This compact hitting-arm position allows her to drive the shot using her rear, left, shoulder, so the power comes naturally from her body rotation.

gives your body the information it needs to hit the shot, and to hit it the same way on every ball. As one student said, "In previous lessons, I was repeatedly told that my preparation was late or that I needed to follow through, but nothing seemed to change. Once I had a visual model of the turn and the finish position, I quickly developed a feel for the stroke."

Advanced players can use the models to correct technical problems in existing strokes. Beginners can use the models to create classical stroke patterns from the ground up. You can use the chapters together or independently to work on one or more individual strokes. The bulk of your effort comes at the start of the Visual Tennis training program. This means that you must take time to master the key positions in the strokes using the various checkpoints, and then translate them into pictures through detailed visualization.

At first, this is more involved than a regular lesson in which the pro gives the first verbal tip and you begin hitting balls immediately. In the long run, however, it is simpler and more powerful. Once you have learned the key positions and key images, your body will have absorbed everything it needs to know to hit the stroke. You can make corrections and improvements by referring to these basic positions. Problems and their solutions become a matter of simple comparison to the familiar elements of a given model stroke.

It may sound simple just to say, "Swing low to high on the forehand," but what does a statement like that really mean? The racket can be in at least four or five positions on the turn, all of which could be considered low. But which, if any, is correct? Where exactly does the racket head point? How far back does it go? In what position is the arm? Where are the shoulders and legs? Visual Tennis models provide answers to such questions.

A picture, it is often said, is worth a thousand words. This is nowhere more true than in tennis. You could fill paragraphs with technical descriptions of the information contained in a single Visual Tennis model image. Because it reduces the number of technical elements required to learn or correct strokes, and conveys this information directly through the body's natural learning process, the Visual Tennis system produces results that are superior to and more quickly learned than those produced by the tennis-tip approach. Using the system you can develop classical stroke patterns with great simplicity, consistency, accuracy, and power.

The goal is not to memorize a long list of technical facts but to develop effective stroke patterns in the simplest and most natural way. The initial teaching progression for each stroke includes at most four steps—the creation of four key physical positions and the corresponding internal mental pictures. Then, by developing and using the stroke keys, we reduce to a single step the process of executing the stroke on court.

Each stroke chapter will guide you through the process of developing the model stroke and the key images. After working with the model and the keys, you go to the final chapter, "Progressive Stroke Development." There you will learn a series of progressive drills and exercises that will allow you to master the execution of the stroke until it is effortless and reliable even under intense competitive pressure.

This sequence of progressive exercises is critical to the success of the training process. In traditional lessons, the student typically receives large numbers of relatively easy balls. The player then jumps directly into competitive match play, and the new stroke usually collapses.

In contrast, Visual Tennis uses a gradual process to build your physical skills, your ability to use visualization, and your confidence so that you can execute strokes under increasing competitive pressure. It begins by teaching you how to build stroke models without hitting balls. As you work on the key positions, you also learn to close your eyes and create corresponding mental images. You then use these images to guide the execution of the stroke and lay the basis for developing the mental game. On court the training process begins with what we call *controlled drill*—working with an even feed of slow- to medium-paced balls. You gradually increase the difficulty of controlled drill as your ability to execute the model increases. At the point where your stroke breaks down, you should temporarily decrease the level of difficulty. Once you recover the ability to execute at the lower level, you should again increase the difficulty.

Controlled drill is also critical because it allows you to learn the process of muscle-memory correction. Muscle-memory corrections are a central part of the Visual Tennis learning process. They allow you to see the exact degree to which you are able to execute the model and correct mistakes, or deviations, as they happen. To do a muscle-memory correction, you learn to freeze at the end of a given stroke, wherever you may be. By freezing in your finish position, you can evaluate the accuracy of the stroke pattern. You do this by comparing your actual finish position to the checkpoints for the model stroke. You then make a muscle-memory correction by physically adjusting from your actual position to the correct position. Finally, you visualize the correction and execute a practice swing according to the corrected model.

Pete Sampras demonstrates the classical, high forehand follow-through. His wrist is at eye level, and the forearm of his hitting arm is at a 45-degree angle to the court.

© Steve Margheim

Muscle-memory work is one of the most powerful aspects of the Visual Tennis process. Correcting muscle memory eliminates another common problem in traditional lessons. This occurs when the student makes a technical mistake and, without correcting it, simply recovers to the ready position. The pro points out the error, but the student makes the same error on the next ball or makes a new error trying to correct the old one. This pattern can repeat itself to the point of absurdity: The pro gives the same tip repeatedly, the player goes back and forth from one error to another, but no fundamental change occurs.

Muscle-memory correction gives the tennis player, and the teaching pro, a way to break this unproductive cycle. As one student said, "Once I understood the model, I could notice where my racket was after I completed a stroke, and then I could self-correct. Previously I would just fall apart and have no idea what was going on, but now I know what I should be doing so I'm able to improve my strokes even on a bad day."

A key step in progressive stroke development is adding basic footwork to controlled drill, according to the Visual Tennis patterns described in the chapter on court movement. The goal is to create patterns of movement that allow you to arrive in a balanced turn position ready to hit the ball as if it had initially come directly to you. As you develop your ability to move and establish this turn position, you should increase the difficulty of the balls and the distance you must move. Again, when the stroke begins to break down, you should revert to the more basic drill and reestablish the model.

After achieving success in controlled drill, you progress to live rallies. Initially, you should try to execute the basic strokes in simple exchanges without large increments of movement. Again, over time, you increase the range of movement until a breakdown occurs. Now you drop down to a more controlled level and reestablish your ability to replicate the model. The next step is to increase ball velocity and vary the speed and the spin of the ball feeds with the basic controlled drill, movement drills, and live rallies.

Before progressing to match play you should test any stroke in what we call *intermediate competitive situations,* for example, playing backcourt point games to four points without serving. This is a critical bridge from training to playing.

An indispensable part of developing your strokes, learning to correct muscle memory, and working your way through the progressive levels of difficulty is seeing your tennis on video. You can accomplish this by using a home video camera, or better, by working with a pro who makes extensive use of video in teaching. No amount of verbal description can replace this direct visual feedback. It communicates to the student in a different medium and creates a clarity that is impossible to achieve otherwise. Students often find regular viewing of themselves on video the most powerful single aspect of the Visual Tennis process. Using video gives you the critical information you need to compare your internal mental imagery to the actual pattern of your strokes.

THE MENTAL GAME

The first component in the Visual Tennis system is the construction and the correction of stroke patterns. The second interrelated component is the development of the mental game. Visual Tennis approaches the strokes and the mental game simultaneously. While you are learning the key positions in the stroke models, you are also laying the groundwork to execute them naturally in competitive play.

Visual Tennis bridges the physical and the mental game by training you to use mental imagery to execute your stroke patterns under pressure. You will learn to reduce the process of executing the stroke to the use of one key image. This image functions as a mental blueprint. On court, you learn to visualize this key image, for example, the image of the finish position on the forehand. With your mind's eye you see the finish position and then simply let the swing pattern cover the projected image. The process can happen in the flash of a second that you have to execute strokes in match play. By visualizing key images in actual play, you learn how to stay positive under pressure and execute winning shots with consistency.

One of the greatest problems most players face in developing the mental game is staying confident in pressure situations. The keys give you a way to flood yourself with positive images and feelings of confidence. If you observe much competitive tennis you know that the easy shots are the ones many players miss most often. The chance to hit a winner, particularly at a crucial point in a match, creates an expectation that in turn raises the fear of missing. The belief that we are going to miss becomes self-fulfilling. Anyone who has played competitive tennis can remember this feeling: You have a short ball, the open court, and a chance to hit a winner on a big point. Something inside tells you that you are going to miss the shot, and that is exactly what happens.

Visual Tennis bridges the physical and the mental game through the use of key positive images. Players can refer to their personal stroke key charts during game changes to correct mistakes and maintain or restore confidence under pressure.

Many players repeat this pattern hundreds or thousands of times, whether they are playing tournaments or weekly club matches. Over time, the consistent inability to hit shots under pressure causes them to brand themselves losers or chokers. Some players become so negative and frustrated that they end up hating the game, or giving it up.

The key images in the Visual Tennis system provide an antidote for this self-destructive cycle. We watch the great players on television hit big shots repeatedly in pressure-packed situations, and we assume that we should be able to do the same. But the ability to perform under pressure is what sets the great players apart. They make shots under pressure, not only because they have the ability, but because they believe that they will. By learning to think in positive images, you can do the same.

Many top players report seeing positive imagery spontaneously in match play. In the words of John McEnroe: "Sometimes in a match I'll suddenly see a shot flash across my mind's eye just before I hit it." Or as Andre Agassi put it: "You have visions of what you are going to do before it happens." Other top players have used imagery systematically. Billie Jean King told me that as a junior player she would see spontaneous images of shots. Later in her career she turned this ability into a conscious process, training herself to visualize a positive image for every ball she hit.

The minds of average players, by contrast, are often filled with conflicting technical information and self-criticism. Following the process of traditional lessons, players attempt to talk themselves through their strokes during matches. Visual Tennis helps turn off this internal verbal dialogue. The system gives players the ability to reprogram their thinking under pressure and to replace negative expectations with positive imagery. By previsualizing positive images, players can create and sustain enthusiasm and confidence. In a literal sense, players learn to see themselves in a new way.

A tournament player who had been ranked in various age and ability divisions over a 20-year period gave this explanation of how the Visual Tennis keying process changed his feelings about the game:

> I'd played competitive tennis my whole life and I'm not sure I ever remember hitting a critical winner under pressure. I'd pretty much decided that I was just a choker, and that the only way to win was just to keep the ball in play. I still won a lot of matches but they were often so emotionally draining I began to question why I was still playing the game. With Visual Tennis, that all started to change. The first thing was just to notice how fearful I really was to hit winning shots. Something inside me just told me I was going to miss. As I started to develop key images and use them on the court, I was amazed. Visualizing that I would make the shot helped me believe in myself. For the first time in my life I started to hit a lot of easy winners. I played matches where I won most of the points instead of just waiting for the other guy to lose. I hit a tough volley for a winner at match point in a tournament final. The feeling was just incredible. I've actually started to look forward to the pressure.

A key image can be any part of the image of the overall stroke. The key can be a still image, or a moving image—a kind of mini-movie of the entire stroke or

© Steve Margheim

On his forehand return, Sampras uses a compact, straight backswing with a small, natural loop to change the direction of the racket. Note the hitting-arm position with the elbow close to the body and the wrist laid back.

of part of the stroke. In the chapters that follow you will learn a series of key images for all the strokes. Chapter 9, "Progressive Stroke Development," will show you how to test them and evaluate which keys are effective, or "active," in your game. Chapter 9 will also show you how to construct a personal stroke key chart for each stroke. The chart lists key images for executing the stroke and for counteracting specific technical tendencies. Building your system of stroke keys is an individual, creative process. It's fun and exciting. You are in control of the process, and your keying system will be unlike anyone else's.

The simple fact is that tennis happens too fast to think about in words. But pictures can flow through the mind at the speed your body moves on the court. You'll learn to look forward to the pressure situations because you will be able to stay positive and make things happen, leading to greater competitive success.

OFFCOURT TRAINING

The third component of the system is the use of Visual Tennis imagery off court—both to strengthen muscle memory of the basic stroke patterns and to improve your ability to use the key images in competitive performance. Offcourt training can provide you the training edge enjoyed by top Olympic and professional athletes.

Many studies over the last two decades have established the positive effect of mental imagery training in sports learning and competition. A prominent researcher in the field, Dr. Richard Suinn (1997), summarized the research on mental practice: "We know for certain mental practice has a powerful effect on performance outcomes." A metanalysis of more than 60 individual studies assessed the effectiveness of imagery on improving physical performance. The conclusion was that across a diverse range of motor skills, visualization by itself—that is, visualization even without physical practice—produced measurable improvements in performance (Feltz and Landers 1985).

Various surveys of Olympic and other elite athletes, coaches, and sport psychologists have found that 85 to 95 percent incorporate some form of imagery into their overall training programs. Legendary champions such as golfer Jack Nicklaus, Olympic skier Jean-Claude Killy, bodybuilder Arnold Schwarzenegger, decathlon gold medalist Bruce Jenner, and all-time great running back Jim Brown, to name only a few, are on record extolling the value of mental imagery and the key role it played in their achievements. Typically, these athletes report that previsualizing their performance and anticipating what could happen in competition was a significant factor in their success. For top athletes imagery training is not an exotic, supplemental training technique. It is fundamental to the way they train and perform. The use of imagery should be a vital, primary element in all sports training programs, including those of tennis players at all levels.

To be truly effective, however, visualization training must first show you how to construct a superior technical mental image of a given stroke. Only then can you benefit from visual practice in a systematic or meaningful way. This is why the majority of this book focuses on construction of technical models and stroke keys. They are the basis for both the oncourt and offcourt training programs in the Visual Tennis system. Once you develop clear models, the systematic use of imagery off court will facilitate the improvement of both your basic strokes and your ability to execute them in competition.

How much visual practice should the average player do away from the court? This is a question that you must answer for yourself based on your experience. As a start, try one brief session of visual practice for every session of actual play. For example, if you play three times a week, have three offcourt visual training sessions.

The simplest procedure for doing offcourt visualizations is to sit in a comfortable chair and close your eyes. Some players prefer to do visual work in a quiet, or even dark, environment. Others do it to music. The important thing is to be relaxed, comfortable, and motivated. If you have trouble sitting still, you may choose to get up and swing the racket while doing the visualizations. Along with this kind of systematic session, it is possible to work on your offcourt imagery almost anywhere when you have the time to focus on your tennis. One student explained that she visualized strokes when taking her afternoon walks: "I also visualize my strokes when I'm at a meeting, but don't mention this to my boss."

Starting with one stroke, see yourself executing it according to the models shown in the individual chapters. Give the image as much detail as you can. Try to see your entire body and your racket. See the brand name on your racket, tennis shoes, tennis clothes, and so forth. Try visualizing in color if you don't normally do so. Visualize the swing at different speeds. Start in slow motion and gradually work up to the speed of your swing in play. Add the sound of the ball striking the center of the sweet spot. Remember to include the kinesthetic aspect by imagining exactly how the motion feels.

Now shift to the system of personal stroke keys you have devised for the stroke. Focus on each key in the context of the overall stroke. Visualize each of your keys. Repeat the procedure for your other strokes. You can visualize shot combinations as well as basic strokes. See yourself hit a forehand, then a backhand, then a forehand, and so on. Visualize patterns of play that are typical of the kinds of points you play or would like to play. For example, visualize yourself working an opponent off the court, crosscourt, with your forehand and hitting a winner down the line. Put points together—a serve followed by a winning first volley, or a return of serve followed by a passing shot. Visualize the combinations that are your strengths, and more important, those that are your weaknesses.

A powerful dimension in offcourt visual training is the use of video images. This means watching video of good stroke technique to reinforce your visual models. Video is also a source of timing, rhythm, and inspiration. *The Winning Edge* is an example of an instructional video designed to enhance visual modeling, as are two Sybervision tapes featuring Stan Smith and Chris Evert. The Sybervision tapes are excellent sources of images of classical technique that are generally compatible with the Visual Tennis models and teaching system. By taping television matches you can tap into an almost limitless source of additional images. Replays that isolate the strokes of top players are particularly useful.

In addition, a video version of Visual Tennis is available. This tape provides clear video models of classical technique and the key images taught within the system. Both tournament and league players have successfully used the Visual Tennis video to prepare themselves mentally for match play. You can put together your five-minute offcourt visualization segments using some or all of these video sources, or using them in different combinations. To keep the process fresh, rotate the imagery often and add new sources when possible.

As part of the offcourt training process, every student should make a personal visual modeling video. Using your home video camera or working with your pro, record a series of perfect practice swings. Now record yourself executing the models by hitting balls in controlled drill, preferably against a ball machine. If possible, edit together the best examples of each stroke. You may choose to set them to music. We have had excellent results putting together these types of tapes for junior players using their favorite music.

Other variations are making video prints from your modeling tapes using a home video printer or taking photos of yourself in the key model positions. You can put them on your bathroom mirror, keep them in your racket bag, or place them in your car for viewing when you are stuck in traffic. Try doing visualization by relying on your mental images in two of three image training sessions and watching video in the other. Start with 5 minutes of visualization or 5 to 10 minutes of video. If you wish, you can build up the number or length of your sessions from there.

A final offcourt training technique is to observe high-level tennis in person or on television. You can consciously re-create the experience that many players report of spontaneously playing better after watching other players. Almost every tennis community has local open tournaments. Study the top players in your area, particularly those with strokes or shot patterns you admire. If there is college tennis in your area, become a fan. College matches are an excellent source for both technical imagery and emotional inspiration. Make going to competitive tennis events a part of your imagery training program. Think of yourself as an active mental participant, not a passive spectator. As you watch players with great strokes, imagine yourself simultaneously hitting the same shots.

Perhaps the most powerful application of offcourt visualization is in specific prematch preparation. Pancho Gonzales, considered by some to be among the greatest players of all time, had a legendary prematch ritual. In the locker room he would sit quietly and visualize the exact patterns and shot combinations he knew he would need to defeat a particular opponent. It usually worked. One student trained in the Visual Tennis system, a good athlete who took up tennis as an adult and became a successful league and ranked tournament player, described his use of prematch imagery this way:

> When I'm preparing to play a match, I use the stroke model to practice mentally. I'll see myself executing a stroke and sense how it feels to model the position. I find myself doing this spontaneously, almost any time of the day.

Using the Visual Tennis system you can also prepare highly specific series of key images for specific competitive situations. A girls' high school team was the underdog in a league championship match. Because he was familiar with the players, the coach knew his team was capable of winning the match. For each singles player and doubles team he prepared a special key sheet with the stroke keys or patterns he thought necessary to win the match. For his number-one singles player, for example, the patterns included frequent net approaches to create cumulative pressure on a talented opponent who had a history of becoming mentally fragile in tough matches.

For his doubles teams, it meant aggressive movement to the middle to poach on the opponents' returns in their service games. The patterns also included solid low returns against serve. Only after forcing the other team to volley up,

John McEnroe: A Visual Tennis Case Study

At the start of 1991 John McEnroe had a problem. In the middle of a final come-back drive, he was convinced he could still compete with the world's top players. For several months, however, his serve—the dominating shot that made him one of the most electrifying players in tennis in the late 1970s and early 1980s—was consistently the weak link in his play. His average first-serve percentage had dropped to less than 50 percent. The first serves he did get in were registering ball speeds in the mid-90-mile-per-hour range on the tour radar guns.

The result was that John had to work hard on his service games, was under constant pressure to hit difficult first volleys, and was often broken twice or three times a set. Though his legendary mental toughness kept him in many matches, he seemed to have lost the firepower to win against top players.

Working with John in making *The Winning Edge* instructional video, I had spent many hours studying his technique, particularly his serve. After watching John play, however, it became clear to me that he had developed a technical problem in his service backswing that was the cause of his loss of consistency and power. We agreed to analyze the changes in his motion and compare it to the glory days of the mid-1980s. We believed that if he could recover the original biomechanics of his motion, he could restore his serving effectiveness and again compete successfully at the highest levels of the game.

When John and I began working together in February 1991, I used the same procedure I had used with hundreds of players at all levels who came to our tennis school with various technical problems. The first step is always identifying the problem to the player visually, using high-speed video.

In John's case, the technical problem was a shift in the path of his backswing. Although John's sideways stance and increased torso rotation were an advance in the biomechanics of serving, his racket windup and the path of his swing had always been perfectly classical.

This meant that although his shoulders and hips started almost parallel to the baseline, his arm and racket stayed in the plane of his shoulders during the windup. As John's arm and racket moved through the windup in the plane of the shoulders, they were therefore parallel to the baseline, until coming up at the start of the racket drop. His motion was fluid, rhythmic, and effortless.

By the end of 1990, however, John had developed a severe deviation in this original motion. His arm and racket were swinging back behind the plane of his body, extending out over the court rather than staying parallel to the baseline. The face of his racket was opening until it was parallel to the court surface. At the most extreme point, John's arm and racket were reaching out over the court by about three feet. Video analysis showed that this change was putting a third- to a half-second delay in his motion. From this awkward position, John was forced to muscle the racket forward to continue the motion, causing a loss of rhythm and momentum, as well as putting pressure on the shoulder joint. When John saw his serve in slow-motion replay, it was the first time I'd ever seen him speechless. Although he was aware that something was seriously impeding his serve, he had no idea what had happened to the shape of his backswing.

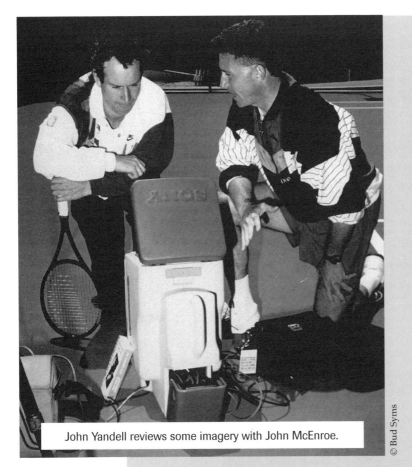

John Yandell reviews some imagery with John McEnroe.

© Bud Syms

After identifying the problem, the next step was the creation of a corrective model. In John's case we had a perfect source—video from *The Winning Edge,* when his serve was the most dominating shot in tennis. With the video system on court, we looked at examples of his service motion that showed the backswing moving freely with the arm and racket in the plane of the shoulders and parallel to the baseline.

We focused on one key image. The arm and racket were in line with the shoulders, parallel to the baseline, and the racket face was square, or perpendicular, to the court surface. I had John stand in position to serve and move through his windup in slow motion until he reached the key position. I had him close his eyes and make a mental image of this model position, and asked him to visualize what this position looked like and felt like inside his mind.

I told him to project that mental image into space behind him like an imaginary template or blueprint, and simply move his arm and racket through the model image we had created. Then I had him move through his motion to this new position with his eyes closed. John understood the process instantly. I stepped back, held my breath, and watched. On his first serve, half of the deviation in the backswing disappeared. Now that was exciting! I knew at that moment that the Visual Tennis process would work for John.

Over the course of the two days on the court, we repeated the elements of the training process. After about four hours on the court—alternating between practice serves, playing points, and video analysis—the deviation in his motion had disappeared. The windup stayed parallel to the baseline, with the racket face perpendicular. The ball was coming off his racket with a noticeably more forceful sound. John asked for a still print of the key image to keep in his racket bag.

The test came that March in Chicago when John played his first tournament since the training. His motion held together beautifully. For the tournament John served 60 percent, with his serve consistently registering in the 108- to 115-mile-per-hour range. He won the event, serving 15 aces in the final. A month later we repeated the two-day training process. But there was little for me to do except shoot video of John, exchange banter, and enjoy watching him work out with his brother Patrick. Every time we checked the serve it was conforming beautifully to the model.

were they to attempt to pass or lob. A week before the match, he instructed his players to spend five minutes a day visualizing the patterns and, if they wished, listening to their favorite music.

On match day his team executed the plan with ferocious precision. At number-one singles, his player approached the net consistently and effectively, winning a 2-hour, three-set match when her opponent drilled a passing shot into the tape on match point. His doubles teams made one successful poach after another, forced volley errors with their consistent returns, and won easily in straight sets. One player described the experience this way: "Before I had even set foot on the court, I had already played the match. As we played, I was hitting the strokes and playing the points just the way I had visualized them."

With the Visual Tennis system you can gain this high-tech training edge. Done properly, offcourt training is exciting and fun. It's a secret weapon that you can use to speed your development, raise your level of play, make tennis a bigger part of your life, and, possibly, create memorable championship performances of your own.

CHAPTER 2

MODELING THE CLASSICAL STYLE

The Visual Tennis system creates a series of stroke models that abstract core elements of the classical style. Across almost a century of tennis history, most of the great champions in the game have used some variation of classical style. In the era before modern professional tennis, the list includes legendary names such as Bill Tilden, Ellsworth Vines, Don Budge, Jack Kramer, Tony Trabert, Ken Rosewall, and John Newcombe, among many others. The list of the premodern era women's classical champions is also illustrious: Alice Marble, Helen Wills Moody, Maureen Connolly, Margaret Court, and Billie Jean King.

With the arrival of open tennis, superstars such as Jimmy Connors, Ivan Lendl, Chris Evert, Martina Navratilova, and Steffi Graf continued to dominate with classical technical style. We can also include in the classical pantheon a player who is one of the purest examples of power, elegance, and versatility in the history of the game, Pete Sampras, who may go down as the greatest men's player of all time. Other great players are ideal models for certain classical strokes. John McEnroe, for example, demonstrates the core technical elements of classical volleys as well as any player in tennis history. The same is true of Andre Agassi's beautiful, minimalist two-handed backhand. Michael Chang and Martina Hingis also share these key classical two-handed technical elements.

The history of tennis shows that classical champions have developed an extremely wide range of strategic and tactical options. In some respects, the games of the great classical players could not be more varied. Chris Evert was the prototype of the ultrasteady, two-handed baseliner. Martina Navratilova was one of the great pure serve-and-volley players. Steffi Graf combines one of the biggest forehands in the history of women's tennis with a defensive one-handed slice on the backhand, yet she still dominates from the backcourt with her unique inside-out style.

Jimmy Connors hit the ball early and very flat, and mixed a devastating backcourt game with aggressive, well-timed net approaches, especially late in his career. Ivan Lendl was known for both power and consistency, a combination that allowed him to win on both hard court and clay. Pete Sampras can attack or defend from the baseline, make transition approaches, play pure serve-and-volley tennis, and mix these elements in an unpredictable and effective all-court game. Despite their divergent styles, the players mentioned above share certain fundamentals that place them within the classical technical tradition. The variations in the strategy and styles of these great champions demonstrate the supreme flexibility of the classical style.

Many top junior players develop a one-dimensional, defensive baseline game based on western grips and heavy topspin. Although this style can produce impressive tournament results, the mental strain often causes players to burn out, quit the game, and end up hating tennis. Developing a classical style will increase the chances a gifted player has for later success. Pete Sampras spent his junior career patiently developing the classical all-court style. He never won a national junior title. In his first year in the boys' 18-and-under division, he ranked only 56th nationally. Three years later he

© Steve Margheim

Pete Sampras prepares for a classical one-handed backhand.

seemed to come out of nowhere to win the U.S. Open at age 19. As Sampras himself says, "I would have liked to have won more in the juniors, but I knew what the benefits would be in the long run. I had to develop a more aggressive, more rounded style of play."

DEVELOPING THE CLASSICAL STYLE

If you aspire to play at the top levels of tennis, your focus should be on developing the game it will take to succeed there, not on achieving short-run competitive results. Although many juniors dream of winning Wimbledon or the U.S. Open, only a few will ever play at the pro level. For most juniors, the classical style will enhance the ability to enjoy tennis for life, to play doubles, and to avoid injury.

The same reasoning applies to adult players at all recreational and competitive levels. Compared with either western or continental style, classical strokes are better suited to developing a flexible, all-court style. Western ground strokes require a far more extreme grip change when going to the net. Players who develop long, looping western-swing patterns rarely, if ever, seem comfortable with the radically different grips and compact technique required to volley effectively. Players with continental grips, by contrast, are often at a severe disadvantage in the backcourt, particularly on the forehand side and on slower court surfaces.

Classical players, on the other hand, can play a combination of attacking and backcourt tennis. This mix of attacking and baseline strategies is called the all-court game. The classical style is much better suited to playing all-court tennis than is continental or western tennis. With classical strokes it is possible to attack or to defend in any combination, with equal success. This is especially true on hard courts, which have become virtually standard in the United States.

Classical strokes give you the ability to hit with consistency, accuracy, and depth. This allows you to develop your own distinctive patterns of play. Classical tennis is not defined by specific patterns of strategy—it gives you a wide range of strategic options. Nor is classical tennis defined by the nature and amount of spin you use. You can hit shots with topspin, with underspin, or flat, and still play classical tennis. You may hit a shot with a moderate degree of topspin or with slightly heavier spin. It is possible to hit the ball on the rise, at the top of the bounce, or as it starts its way down. Most recreational players, even most tournament players, will naturally tend to hit the ball as it drops, but there are exceptions at all levels. Classical tennis permits you to experiment with the timing of your strokes to find what works best for you.

The goal in using the Visual Tennis system is to develop versatility within the parameters of your natural abilities. Against some opponents, all-court players should take the net at almost any opportunity. They should play others primarily from the backcourt. Most matches, however, require you to mix the two styles depending on the situation. You should seek to use your relative strengths against the relative weaknesses of each opponent, and choose strategy for its effectiveness against a given opponent, on a given court, on a given day.

A second advantage of the classical style for the average player is that it is biomechanically simple. Classical strokes are simpler to learn and more quickly developed to a higher skill level. Classical patterns contain fewer variables than a game based on continental and western grips. Both the continental and the western-style ground strokes require significant internal motion with the hitting arm, including the release of the wrist over the course of the swing and follow-through. Typically, the shape and length of the swings exhibit much greater variety from one ball to the next, depending on height, depth, and spin. The variations in the technical elements of the basic stroke patterns require a high level of hand-eye coordination to execute consistently, and usually require more development time.

In contrast, the classical patterns in the Visual Tennis system have fewer variables to master. The sequences have simpler swing patterns that eliminate internal arm and wrist motion. Players at any level can develop them more quickly. Beginners can rapidly achieve consistent stroke production using the system. Experienced players can use the models to eliminate technical problems that may have plagued them for years.

CORE CLASSICAL ELEMENTS IN THE VISUAL TENNIS MODELS

The Visual Tennis models are constructed from technical elements common to classical strokes. When variation is possible for parts of a given stroke, such as the shape or timing of the backswing, the models present the simplest version, the one that the majority of players will find the easiest to master and the most effective.

The models include several core elements:

1.   The first element is a classical, eastern forehand grip that places most of the palm of the hand directly behind the racket head. This is combined with an eastern backhand grip for the one-handed backhand, which rotates the palm to the top of the frame. For the two-handed backhand, the grip with the top hand is the same classical forehand, combined with the eastern backhand grip with the bottom hand. (Grips are discussed in Chapter 3.)

2.   The models use immediate, simple preparation on the ground strokes, the volleys, and the overhead. This move is a body-unit turn, initiated with the feet and shoulders. On the volleys this turn move automatically prepares the racket with no additional arm motion or backswing. On the ground strokes, a small, additional straight backswing completes the preparation. This principle of compact preparation will lead automatically to the development of small, elliptical loops without conscious thought or effort.

3.   The models employ simple, unchanging hitting-arm positions. At the completion of the preparation, you set the arm and racket in a specific hitting-arm position. This position remains unchanged through the swing and at the finish. You also set the plane of the racket face at the completion of the preparation. This angle, for example, perpendicular to the court on a topspin drive, also remains unchanged during the swing. The hitting-arm position does not vary through the course of the stroke.

4.   Highly specific finish positions are another key element. Clear checkpoints ensure smooth, consistent finishes. A stroke pattern that is correct at both the turn and the finish—with the hitting arm and the plane of the racket in set, unchanging positions—guarantees that the stroke will be correct at the critical moment of contact.

© Gus Bower

Chris Evert's forehand finish position follows the classical model.

5.   The models use the shoulders and legs to generate power and spin. If the turn, racket preparation, and finish are all correct, the shoulders and legs will uncoil naturally through the course of the stroke, maximizing body leverage and generating power and spin automatically.

The teaching progressions for the models reduce each stroke to four or fewer key positions. The first key position, the ready position, is the same for all ground strokes and volleys. This reduces the number of steps to three at most as you progress from one stroke to the next. On the backhand, we present models for the one-handed topspin backhand, the one-handed slice backhand variation, and the two-handed backhand. The chapter on net play includes models that teach you to hit both flat and with underspin, as well as models for the two-handed backhand volley and the overhead. Each chapter discusses how to decide which model or models you should incorporate into your game.

You can use these building blocks to restructure existing strokes or construct new ones from the ground up. After you establish or correct the pattern, Visual Tennis simplifies the stroke even more by reducing it to a single key image. You then learn to execute the entire stroke pattern in competitive play by visualizing this key. The idea is to make learning and playing great tennis as easy as "one, two, three" and, eventually, as simple as "one."

To complete the unit turn and establish the hitting-arm positions in a compact and direct manner, the Visual Tennis models use straight backswings. At the pro level, you see many backswing variations even among so-called classical players—the circular backswing of Graf, the closed-face motion of Sampras, or the straight backswings of players such as Jimmy Connors or Chris Evert. All these variations have a critical factor in common—they deliver the arm and racket to the classical hitting-arm position before the racket head starts forward to the ball.

For the average player, using the loop backswing makes achieving the proper hitting-arm position far more difficult and often leads to severe problems. Players at lower levels who use the circular loop tend to rely on an exaggerated swing with little shoulder turn or leg action. Some argue that a circular loop is critical to generating racket-head speed. But when we look at top classical players we see that few have ever had large circular loops and that some of the greatest forehands in the game have had straight backswings. Top players initiate the preparation or turn move with the body and the unit turn, not the arm.

Teaching the loop causes similar problems on the backhand side. A common and debilitating problem in hitting the one-handed backhand is the so-called elbow lead, in which the elbow and hand arrive at the contact point before the racket head. Besides preventing the development of a solid basic stroke, this problem contributes to the development of tennis elbow. The loop backswing begins with a large bend in the elbow. This guarantees that the hitting arm will never reach the correct hitting position, which for the one-handed backhand is straight at the contact with the elbow and wrist locked.

Ironically, the use of the simple straight backswing leads automatically to the creation of small elliptical loops as the racket changes direction, loops which maintain the correct hitting-arm position. The human body will automatically introduce a compact circular motion to change direction of a tennis racket as it moves from one position to another. You can't help doing this even if you try— it's something that your body just does. The information the body needs to hit the forehand, or any other stroke, is a clear image of the key positions in a stroke. Once it knows these it will move naturally between them. These positions are what the models provide.

On the basic forehand and backhand drives, classical strokes are based on vertical swing paths. This means the racket head stays vertical, or perpendicular, to the court surface throughout the swing. In contrast, the western or continental forehand often turns over the racket face radically during the follow-through. With a vertical swing plane, the stroke produces topspin naturally and automatically. By making only a minor adjustment in the path of the racket, you can vary the topspin.

From the turn position in the classical ground-stroke patterns, the racket moves upward naturally through the contact so that the vertical racket face brushes across the back side of the ball. This causes the ball to rotate with topspin automatically. By making slight adjustments in the angle of the swing plane, you can vary the amount of topspin at will, without making any fundamental change in the shape of the swing. You can increase topspin to cause the ball to dip more rapidly on a passing shot, or you can increase shot velocity, hitting the ball harder, flatter, and deeper.

On the one-handed slice backhand and on underspin volleys, the racket generates spin in the same way. You set the angle of the racket face at the completion of the preparation. This angle remains unchanged through the stroke. Hitting underspin or slice is greatly simplified—the angle of the racket face generates the spin as it moves through the swing plane.

Many students ask why they should worry about follow-through when the ball is already off the strings. The answer is that follow-through determines the direction and speed of racket movement at contact. A full follow-through maximizes racket-head acceleration and produces consistency in the natural course of the stroke. These finish positions also guarantee proper body rotation over the course of the stroke and automatically produce maximum power. If you prepare the stroke correctly at the

© Steve Margheim

Pete Sampras begins to rotate into his serve.

turn and execute the model finish with precision, you will generate natural power. Your hips and shoulders will rotate a full 90 degrees, and your legs will simultaneously uncoil.

Another confusing topic in tennis theory is the position and role of the legs in the ground strokes and the relative merits of the open and closed stances. The basic Visual Tennis models employ traditional closed stances. By using the closed stance as a basic pattern, you will find it much easier to master the core elements of shoulder rotation, hitting-arm position, and follow-through. After you learn how to use the closed stance, you should develop the ability to hit from the open stance on both sides. The chapter on court movement shows how to position yourself to the ball so that you can execute the same technical swing pattern off either the front or back foot.

In the chapter on serving, Visual Tennis presents a simple progression for using the legs to maximize power and spin on the serve. Virtually every top player uses the same pattern of coiling the legs in the motion. This drives the player into the air so that he or she lands in the court on the front foot while the back foot moves back away. This pattern is universal in pro tennis, but traditional lessons almost never teach it. Visual Tennis will teach you how to create the same pattern to generate natural and effortless power.

In addition, Visual Tennis presents a new way for you to increase power in the serve by automatically increasing shoulder rotation. Players such as John McEnroe and Pete Sampras have taken the role of the shoulders in the serve to a new level. For the first time, Visual Tennis shows how players at any level can alter their starting stance to create the same effect without any change in the basic motion.

The models present the elements that classical strokes have in common but do not address elements of personal style. Players at every level, including the great champions mentioned above, will develop unique personal strokes and match strategies. Despite core similarities, no two classical players have ever looked or played the game exactly alike.

Teachers and players who study the strokes of champions often focus on idiosyncrasies rather than the underlying fundamentals. They end up copying things that are irrelevant or even detrimental to their tennis. Raising the sole of your front foot briefly at the start of the service motion the way Pete Sampras does will do nothing to improve your serve. Developing the same classical racket-head path and learning to use your legs and body rotation for power as Sampras does will maximize your serving effectiveness for life. It is a bad idea to copy the timing of Steffi Graf's forehand by waiting until after the bounce of the ball to begin the motion of your arm in the swing. Instead, you should emulate the classical hitting-arm position and high follow-through that Graf employs once her motion begins.

If you observe players trained in the Visual Tennis system, you will see that their strokes share the basic technical elements presented here. Although no two look exactly alike, their strokes are highly reliable and effective. Differences between players in body proportion, strength and flexibility, and temperament and strategic style lead to natural variation in the length and shape of the swing, and the amount of body rotation, spin, and pace. The Visual Tennis models give you many options in developing a unique strategic style and interpretation of the all-court game. And this is the way it should be.

Players should understand that the models presented here are just that—models, archetypes, or guides. We have designed the models to teach players at all levels how to develop core classical elements. They present the ideal form of the elements that students should strive to approximate. Their great value is that they give players a precise image and a precise feeling of what they are trying to do. By learning to approximate the stroke models, players can develop their full potential for the game, learn to play their best tennis consistently, and enjoy the game for life!

CHAPTER 3

VISUAL TENNIS GRIPS

© Steve Margheim

The grip is the foundation for developing the classical stroke patterns in the Visual Tennis system. Small changes in hand position on the racket can have significant consequences in the shape, comfort, and effectiveness of the stroke patterns. The effect of these changes can vary among players. Many players with technical problems in their swings come to the Visual Tennis system with some version of the classical grips and can progress directly to the stroke models. If you have questions about your grips, or if you are a beginner, this chapter outlines how to develop the grip that will work best with each of the Visual Tennis stroke patterns.

VISUAL TENNIS FOREHAND GRIP

The central characteristic of the Visual Tennis forehand grip is that it places the palm of the hand in line with the face of the racket. This means that when you close your hand around the racket, most of your palm is on the *back* bevel of the handle. This palm position allows you to hit through the shot with your wrist laid back. A core element in the classical forehand is using the palm to drive the racket face, with the hitting arm set in a double-bend position throughout the stroke. This grip increases your ability to push the racket head with the palm while eliminating the wrist as a variable. It means that the leverage from your shoulders and legs will automatically be increased.

To get the forehand grip, hold the racket by the throat with your *left* hand (assuming you are right-handed). Place your *right* palm flat on the face of the strings and simply slide your palm down along the shaft of the racket to the grip. Now close your hand around the grip and

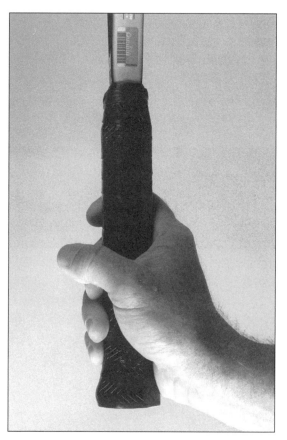

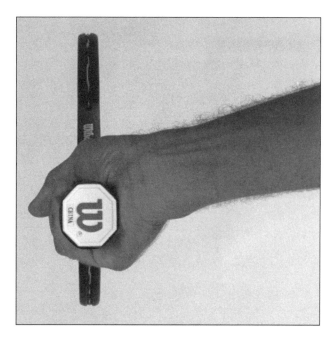

shake hands with the racket. The top finger, the index finger, should be spread slightly from the rest of the fingers.

The key checkpoints for determining whether your grip is correct are the position of the heel pad of your hand and the position of your index knuckle. Place your heel pad squarely on the side bevel of the handle, that is, in a plane parallel to the racket face. Align the knuckle of your index finger in the center of this same side bevel.

Although the Visual Tennis variation of the classical forehand grip will work best for most players, there are exceptions. If you are currently comfortable with a grip that varies slightly from the model grips, I would advise trying to develop or improve your stroke pattern without making a change. Often a player can create an effective pattern with a grip that is shifted slightly from the pattern presented here. For example, Martina Navratilova hit a beautiful classic forehand with a grip rotated slightly toward the continental grip. In contrast, in his forehand grip, Ivan Lendl rotated his palm slightly underneath the handle toward the western grip.

VISUAL TENNIS ONE-HANDED BACKHAND GRIP

To hit the one-handed backhand, you must change the grip at the beginning of the stroke. To do this, rotate your racket hand to the left, toward the top of the frame, until your heel pad is resting squarely on the top bevel. The second, or lower, knuckle of your index finger should now be in line with the center of the top *right* bevel. This places most of the palm on the top bevel of the grip.

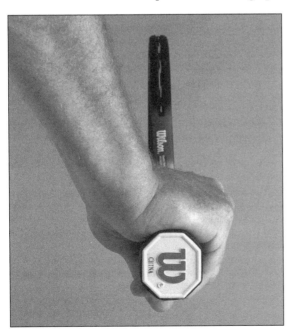

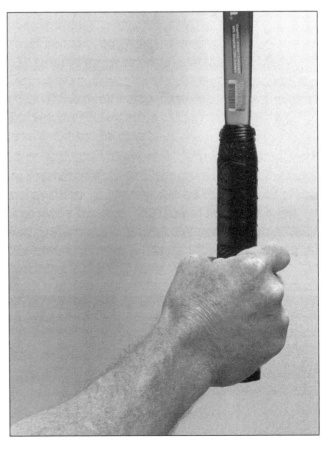

As with the forehand, you may use slight variations in developing the Visual Tennis one-handed backhand. Some classical players rotate the hand slightly farther so the index knuckle is verging on the top bevel. Usually, this will cause the player to generate slightly more topspin when executing the pattern. If you are comfortable with the way you hold the racket, try developing the model with this slightly stronger grip. If you have trouble hitting through the ball or controlling the shot, adjust the grip more precisely to the Visual Tennis model. The stronger grip may also make it more difficult to hit through the ball with slice. Players often must experiment with slight changes to determine the most comfortable and effective variation.

The eastern backhand grip will work for hitting the ball flat, with topspin, or with slice. When hitting slice, however, more advanced players may eventually shift the grip slightly to the continental (explained later). This will allow them to drive through the ball more directly on the backhand side when hitting with underspin. Although it involves adding an additional grip change, you may want to experiment with the continental if you hit your slice backhand consistently long or if it tends to float and lack pace.

VISUAL TENNIS TWO-HANDED BACKHAND GRIPS

The two-handed backhand uses the same forehand grip with the *top* hand, demonstrated earlier. To achieve this, place your *left* hand (assuming you are right-handed) on the face of the strings. Slide it down along

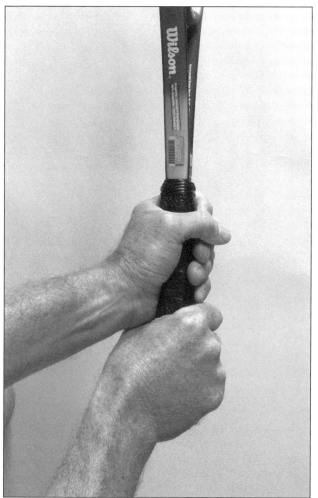

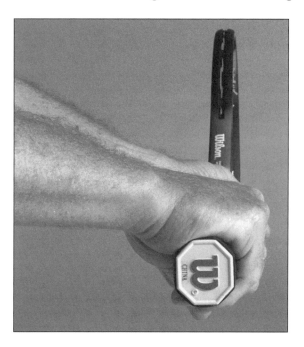

the shaft of the racket and onto the grip until your hands are touching but not overlapping. Close the fingers of your left hand around the racket handle. Again, your heel pad and index knuckle should be in the middle of the back-side bevel of the racket.

You can combine this grip with the regular forehand grip on the bottom, or dominant, hand. But it is preferable to shift this grip to an eastern backhand, as shown previously, to promote the development of slice as you progress as a player.

VISUAL TENNIS CONTINENTAL GRIP

The continental grip is approximately halfway between the classical forehand and backhand grips. This means that the heel pad of the racket hand is *partially* on top of the top bevel of the racket frame. This is the ideal grip for hitting spin on the volleys and on the serve.

On the volley, the continental grip allows you to come under the ball with natural underspin without having to distort the stroke pattern. With the classical forehand grip, however, you cannot accomplish this without moving the racket head more sharply down under the ball, particularly on low volleys, which you must hit with underspin. A similar downward action is required to hit a slice on the backhand volley with the classical eastern backhand grip.

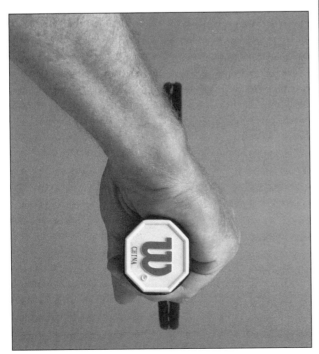

By comparison, the continental grip will produce underspin automatically on both volleys without the need to alter the path of the racket head. The continental grip also has the advantage of allowing you to volley on both sides without changing grips. As mentioned earlier, some players may find they are able to drive the ball with slice more solidly by using the continental grip on the one-handed backhand ground stroke as well.

As we will discuss in the chapter "Playing the Net," it is important first to learn to hit the volleys with the same grips you use for ground strokes. You should initially hit the ball flat until your biomechanics are solid. Only then should you experiment with the continental grip. Some players never get comfortable with the continental grip on the forehand volley, and others find it becomes natural quickly. This is not a clear-cut choice. You should make this decision by experimenting.

For most players, the continental grip is also ideal on the serve. Beginners should learn the service motion with the forehand grip. After they develop solid biomechanics, they should switch to the continental. This grip will cause the racket head to approach the ball at an angle, producing spin automatically, or with only a small adjustment to the swing pattern. Some players use a more extreme eastern backhand grip on the serve, and it is possible to develop a classical motion with this grip as well. If you are comfortable with this grip, you can use it in working with the serve model. Many players, however, particularly below the highest levels, will find it difficult and awkward.

To make solid contact with this grip, you must learn to rotate your forearm more radically outward as it comes up toward the ball. Some players simply lack the range of motion in the joints to do this successfully. With the continental grip, the spin develops more naturally within the context of the swing pattern used on the basic serve. The only change is using the forearm to vary slightly the angle the racket head approaches the ball. Some players using the eastern grip will hit too much around the side of the ball, generating excessive spin and losing pace. Even those who learn to produce the severe topspin possible with this grip often sacrifice too much pace. If this is the case with your serve, you should experiment with a shift to the continental grip.

CHAPTER 4

THE FOREHAND

The forehand is the most basic shot in tennis, the stroke every player learns first. Most players develop a consistent forehand fairly quickly, and it becomes their best shot. As players progress to higher levels of play, however, the forehand sometimes seems to deteriorate or become less reliable. Usually this occurs because playing at higher levels exposes underlying problems in the stroke pattern.

The forehand is a primary weapon in the classical style. A good forehand should be consistent, accurate, and powerful. If the core technical elements are correct, you can hit the classical forehand with great depth, produce shots with varying pace and spin, and execute winners, passing shots, and approaches reliably and effortlessly under pressure. In this chapter, you will learn how to develop your forehand by using key elements from the Visual Tennis model to restructure your stroke pattern or construct it from the ground up.

FOREHAND CORE ELEMENTS

Although developing a functional forehand may be easy for most players, developing the full potential of the shot and executing it well at a high level of play require a precise biomechanical sequence. You must turn your shoulders sideways, or perpendicular, to the net at the completion of the preparation and then rotate them forward 90 degrees during the swing. To increase body leverage on the ball, you must rotate in a precise sequence. Creating this leverage also requires a specific hitting-arm position—a position rarely discussed in traditional lessons. Few players naturally develop this position, but all the great classical players display it. The higher the level of play, the more important becomes the role of shoulder rotation and corresponding arm position in controlling the shot and generating ball velocity.

Another core element in the classical forehand is the *timing* of the preparation to position the shoulders and hitting arm. Most players are far too slow in initiating the preparation. Slow preparation makes it impossible to achieve full shoulder turns or a consistent hitting-arm position. Without immediate preparation, many players are incapable of executing the stroke when they have to cover the whole court or when they play opponents who have higher ball velocity. Without an immediate full turn, players are unable to increase the contribution of the legs in creating power and spin.

Immediate preparation is a core element in the Visual Tennis forehand model. Using the training progressions you will initiate and complete the preparation as the ball crosses to your side or, at the latest, before the ball bounces. This timing is a key element in developing the classical style.

Players who do not develop these core biomechanical elements and the corresponding timing of the preparation end up using the arm and wrist to hit the forehand. Their strokes tend to have too much internal hitting-arm motion. The shape of their swings fluctuates significantly from ball to ball, particularly when they try to hit with topspin or try to hit a winner or a forcing shot.

If we look at the forehands of great classical players—Pete Sampras, Ivan Lendl, Steffi Graf, and Chris Evert—we see that their strokes maximize body leverage from the shoulders and legs and minimize the role of the arm and wrist. By positioning your body correctly at the turn using the Visual Tennis models, you will generate maximum body leverage automatically as you execute the rest of the swing pattern. Your shoulders, hips, and legs will uncoil and provide natural power and spin without conscious or mechanical effort.

Classical Hitting-Arm Position

After establishing the turn position, you should next focus on hitting-arm position. The foreswing on a classical forehand is best described as a pushing motion with the palm of the hand. With the classical grip the palm and the racket head align naturally. As the motion starts forward from the turn position, the palm pushes the racket all the way through the shot to the finish. To execute the foreswing, you must set up the hitting arm in a specific position as the racket head starts forward to the ball. Your elbow is tucked in toward the waist, and your wrist is laid back. Your arm stays in this double-bend position throughout the swing—at contact and through the finish.

This hitting-arm position allows you to push the racket head through the stroke with your palm. For the top classical-style players, the hitting arm moves into this position at the completion of the preparation, before the racket starts forward to the ball. Pushing the racket with your palm from the turn to the finish with the hitting arm in the correct position guarantees that you will drive the forehand with maximum hip and shoulder rotation. It also ensures that you will make contact in front of the plane of your body. This leads automatically to a compact swing pattern in which your arm and body work together to produce effortless power. It eliminates the common errors of using too large a backswing or producing a wild, uncontrolled follow-through.

Role of the Finish

All great classical players have smooth, high finishes on the forehand, with the wrist reaching approximately eye level. The length of the follow-through naturally maximizes racket-head acceleration at contact. The high finish is also a key to the great aesthetic pleasure players feel when hitting a good classical forehand. This finish position is precise, with little variation from ball to ball.

By establishing the double-bend hitting-arm position and pushing the racket head through the shot with your palm, you are able to generate *natural topspin*. You can also vary the spin by making a small adjustment to increase or decrease

Steve Margheim

Andre Agassi establishes a balanced turn position behind the ball.

how much the racket face brushes the ball. You should generate topspin by using your palm. Hold your wrist in the laid-back hitting position to control how much the racket head brushes the ball. There is no need to shift the overall shape of the swing pattern.

Use of the Wrist

Traditional lessons offer two contradictory views on the position and use of the wrist. A common tip advises players to keep a firm wrist on the forehand. Another tip advocates that the wrist *should* break or release, even on a stroke with an eastern grip, to generate spin or racket-head speed. Neither view describes the wrist position on a technically superior classical forehand, and both ignore the relationship of the wrist to the overall position of the hitting arm.

Keeping a firm wrist implies that the arm and racket stay straight in line. This makes the contact late or behind the front edge of the body, stiffens the swing, causes the player to muscle the ball, and reduces the ability to generate power and spin. Releasing the wrist during contact has a similar effect: It reduces the leverage coming from body rotation and makes the arm the primary source of power. By releasing the wrist the player is less able to keep the racket face perpendicular at contact, which reduces shot control.

If the wrist releases at all in the classical pattern, it occurs as a natural and automatic relaxation response as the player completes the technical swing pattern, that is, after the racket passes through the model finish position. The only exceptions are when the player is pulled wide and must stretch simply to get the racket on the ball, or when a player hits topspin on a short or low ball.

Anyone who has the opportunity to see high-speed video of good classical forehands will agree that the ball is long gone from the racket face before *any* wrist movement occurs. At contact the wrist is always laid back. It stays in this position until well after the hit, usually all the way through the completion of the stroke. The players with great classical forehands all pass through this finish position, or approximate it very closely, on most of their strokes. The length and precision of their strokes are amazing given the supersonic ball speeds of modern professional tennis. Using the model, you can learn to develop precise finishes that produce both power and consistency.

Classical Swing Plane

A basic characteristic of a good classical forehand is a vertical swing plane. The racket face stays perpendicular to the court surface throughout the swing. The racket face must be vertical, or within a few degrees of vertical, at the contact point for the ball to go over the net and into the court. The racket must also be in a vertical position to generate topspin. The hitting-arm position in the classical model presented here sets up this vertical position automatically at the turn. The racket face then stays at the same angle all the way to the finish position. This guarantees it will be vertical at the critical point of contact. The model stroke presents these minimalistic elements, creating a pattern that is easy to learn and easy to execute in play. Even on his famous running forehand, Pete Sampras keeps the plane of the racket face perpendicluar to the court all the way through the finish.

Many good classical players at all levels, Sampras among them, "wrap" the racket over the shoulder after passing through the finish position. This wrapping motion is not part of the technical stroke model presented here. The so-called wrap finish is a consequence, rather than a cause, of a well-executed technical forehand, similar to "pronation" on the serve, as we will see later. This distinction between cause and effect is critical in constructing the models.

The wrap is a relaxation response that results naturally from a sound classical motion, particularly at higher levels of play with greater ball speeds. It will occur on its own if the stroke pattern is correct and the racket acceleration is great enough. But it is a mistake to incorporate it into the technical model or attempt to produce it mechanically. A conscious effort to wrap the finish invariably leads players to cut short the movement of the racket head through the line of the shot, so they fail to reach the true technical finish position. Players trained to wrap typically develop late contact points and hit short with only a fraction of their potential power.

Shape of the Backswing

Another controversial topic in teaching is the proper shape of the backswing on the forehand stroke. The Visual Tennis models initiate the turn motion with the feet and the shoulders. This turning motion alone produces most of the racket preparation. You complete the remainder of the preparation with a simple, straight backswing. This places your hitting arm directly into the classical hitting position at the completion of the preparation. This compact and simple method achieves a biomechanically superior turn position.

A popular opposing view teaches an independent, circular backswing with the arm. This approach is allegedly superior because, with the loop, the racket head is in continuous motion. It travels in a circular path that generates unbroken racket-head acceleration toward ball contact.

For many players, starting the motion with this circular looping action produces disastrous results. Players who learn to begin the motion with an immediate, independent loop with the arm inevitably exaggerate the size of the loop. Focusing on the loop, they also tend to neglect the crucial positioning of the shoulders during the preparation. Lacking natural body leverage from a sound turn position, they compensate with more arm motion and an even larger loop. As the backswing becomes larger it becomes more time consuming. The result is often a gigantic swing with late contact. The player flails at the ball with the arm and wrist and hits an inconsistent forehand with reduced power.

The Visual Tennis model eliminates these potential problems. The initial turn with the straight backswing automatically positions the body and creates the classic hitting-arm position. Beginners feel the strength of this position almost immediately. It sets the stage for developing the other core elements in the classical stroke pattern. Players who have struggled with their forehands for years are amazed at the change in their stroke when they repattern it according to the model presented here.

If you closely observe players such as Chris Evert or Jimmy Connors, two great champions with compact classical forehands and straight backswings, you will

© Steve Margheim

No matter what shape the backswing, classical players establish this double-bend position at the start of the foreswing.

notice something else of interest: Although the backswing is beautifully compact, the racket head never stops moving. The racket traces a small elliptical loop as it changes direction from backward to forward. Using the straight backswing in the Visual Tennis forehand model, you will naturally develop this minimal looping motion, which preserves racket-head speed and automatically facilitates rhythm and timing. The alleged advantage of the circular backswing, that it alone keeps the racket in continuous motion, is an illusion.

Every top player starts the forehand with a unit turn with the shoulders and the feet, not the arm. This is true even for players who have some version of a circular backswing. If you study slow-motion video of Pete Sampras or Steffi Graf, for example, you will see that their bodies are completely perpendicular to the net *before* the movement of the arm begins. Despite the differing shapes of the backswings, both Graf and Sampras also deliver the racket to the precise, classical hitting-arm position at the start of the foreswing. The Visual Tennis model achieves this with the simple straight-back motion. There is no doubt that Graf generates incredible racket-head speed with the unique timing of her circular loop. With her body turned, she unleashes the swing at the last possible instant. Because of her delayed timing, the speed of the swing *must* be extremely fast to get to the contact point. This helps generate her extraordinary velocity.

Sampras's usual backswing on his forehand is a closed-face loop, in which he turns the racket face down toward the court at the start of the loop, in much the same fashion as the forehand of the great Ivan Lendl. But Sampras's backswing, like Graf's, puts the racket and arm in the classic hitting arm position before the foreswing. Establishing this position is a critical element in good preparation. Doing so takes precedence over any potential advantage gained from a delayed looping motion.

We can see this in Sampras's forehand when he is pressed for time. Although Sampras hits most forehands with the closed-face loop, in two situations he uses a straight backswing that is identical to the Visual Tennis model. He uses a straight backswing for his forehand return against a high-velocity first serve and when he is pressed on his famed running forehand. This simpler, more compact version of the Sampras forehand conforms perfectly to the Visual Tennis model.

Open and Closed Stances

Two other technical issues can confound the description of a classical forehand and bear on the creation of the models. Both issues have to do with the feet. The first concerns the so-called open stance. Many top players, including classical technical players like Sampras, hit some or most of their forehands off the back foot. The classical model you will develop gives you the ability to hit off either foot. The key to this flexibility is learning the principles of alignment and balance detailed in the chapter on court movement.

Often overlooked in the debate of open stance versus closed stance are the other key biomechanical elements in the stroke. Players like Sampras and Agassi, who hit many forehands off the back foot, use complete shoulder turns with the line of the shoulders perpendicular to the net, whether hitting with the front foot open or closed. The technical shape of the swing and the hitting-arm position also remain unchanged. Many players who try to hit with an open stance fail to develop these basic elements. They also tend to overrotate the torso through the hit, contact the ball late, and finish inconsistently.

In the initial learning process you will find it easier to master the core biomechanics of the model by using the closed stance. The teaching progression demonstrates the closed stance as the basic pattern. After you have developed the basic model, you can experiment with the open stance as you work on your footwork. You can learn when and how to apply it in your game, following the imagery in the chapter on court movement.

The second issue regarding footwork is the tendency of many great players to leave the ground during the stroke. Some observers believe that players make a conscious effort to jump as they hit. As with many other disputed parts of the game, what we see when a top player leaves the court is an effect rather than a cause. The player generates such force that he or she is literally pulled up off the court.

We can see this in Pete Sampras's forehand, or Andre Agassi's backhand, or the ground strokes of Jimmy Connors on both sides. The effect stems from the superior biomechanics of their strokes. No pro player makes a deliberate effort to jump through the strokes. Those who try to emulate them by jumping as they hit end up destroying the sequencing of their biomechanics. As you develop the classical forehand pattern, strive to execute it by using the model and the keys. If you have the requisite natural ability and create a biomechanically superior classical stroke, you may end up "flying" as well, but you won't have to try to do it.

In the following sections, a combination of text and a sequence of photos abstract the core technical elements you will use to create a precise physical and visual model of the classical forehand. First, the chapter presents the entire stroke sequence. Within this sequence, four key positions are identified. Using the key positions, you will build a stroke that can be consistent and powerful at any level of play. The forehand model uses the Visual Tennis forehand grip or slight variations. If you have questions about whether your grip will work in creating the model, you should first consult chapter 3, "Visual Tennis Grips."

The four key positions are

1. the ready position,
2. the turn or preparation,
3. the contact point, and
4. the finish position.

These four building blocks create the model. The application of each key position to common technical problems is also explained. Experienced players who want to correct technical errors or improve the effectiveness of their forehands should begin by comparing their strokes to the model. This analysis will allow you to determine which key position or positions to focus on. The most effective method is to video your stroke. By watching a video in slow-motion replay you can quickly identify where your swing pattern deviates from the model.

FOREHAND STROKE SEQUENCE

After the sequences, the chapter presents a series of images for learning to execute your forehand in match play. Once you have worked through the teaching progressions and the key images, you should read chapter 9, "Progressive Stroke Development." This will show you a series of progressive drills, exercises, offcourt visualizations, and competitive games that will allow you to develop the full potential of your forehand and learn to hit it consistently under pressure in match play.

VISUAL TENNIS FOREHAND MODEL

Above is the stroke sequence for the Visual Tennis forehand, demonstrating the core elements in all great classical forehands. Note the role of the shoulders in the preparation and execution of the stroke, the compact hitting-arm position, and the high smooth finish. By developing the physical and mental models of these simple key positions, you create the building blocks for your own great classical forehand and the mental toughness to execute it under pressure. You can use the key positions to develop the entire stroke, or use one or more of these positions to correct your own specific problems, as outlined in the following section.

If you observe each of the frames above in the overall stroke pattern, you will also see that passing through each of them correctly will guarantee that the entire swing pattern is correct. If the swing is correct at the ready position, at the turn, at the contact point, and at the finish position, it will *have* to be correct at every point in between.

Forehand Key Positions

The following section illustrates the four key positions for mastering the building blocks of the Visual Tennis forehand. Use the four numbered checkpoints for the shoulders, hitting arm, racket, and legs, to create the physical model for each position and a corresponding kinesthetic image of how each position looks and feels inside your mind's eye. This should be done without the ball. Work until you can execute the swing pattern naturally and automatically without the ball, passing accurately through each of the key positions. Take the time at the start of your work to become comfortable with the checkpoints and you will find that you will develop the stroke rapidly and effortlessly on the court.

FOREHAND KEY POSITIONS

Key Position 1: Ready Position

1. **Shoulders:** Your shoulders are parallel to the net in the ready position. Your upper body is straight up and down from the waist. The bend is in your knees, not at your waist.

2. **Hitting arm:** Your hitting arm is already in the classic, double-bend position. Your elbow is tucked in toward the waist, and your wrist is slightly laid back.

3. **Racket:** The racket is slightly below waist level. It points directly at the net, with the face of the racket perpendicular to the court surface.

4. **Legs:** Your legs are slightly wider than shoulder-width. Your knees are flexed and your weight is slightly forward on the balls of your feet.

Close your eyes and, with as much detail as possible, visualize yourself in the correct ready position. Notice how the position feels. Make the image and the feeling correspond in your mind.

Work with the key image of the ready position if

1. you feel slow getting the motion started,
2. you feel off balance when hitting the stroke, or
3. you have problems recovering for the next shot.

Key Position 2: Turn Position

1. **Shoulders:** Your shoulders have rotated 90 degrees, moving from parallel to the net to perpendicular to the net. Your left shoulder is pointing directly at the net. Your left arm has turned naturally with your shoulders. Your head is turned to follow the oncoming ball.

2. **Hitting arm:** Your hitting arm has rotated with the shoulders. Only a small additional straight backswing is required to finish the preparation. Your elbow is tucked in toward the waist, and your wrist is laid back. The classical hitting-arm position naturally places the racket slightly below waist level.

3. **Racket:** The racket has traveled straight back along a line until the head points directly at the back fence. The shaft of the racket is parallel to the court. The butt of the racket is visible to the opponent, and the face of the racket is still perpendicular to the court.

4. **Legs:** You have stepped or pivoted sideways with both feet and have pointed them to the side fence. Your shoulders and legs have worked together to produce this simple unit-turn position. Your weight is on the right, or pivot, foot. The toes of your left foot provide balance. Your knees are still flexed.

Move from the ready position to the turn. Establish the position physically using the checkpoints and then create the visual image. Close your eyes and visualize with detail how the position looks and feels.

Work with the key image of the turn if

1. your preparation is consistently late,
2. your shot lacks power, or
3. you have trouble hitting topspin.

FOREHAND KEY POSITIONS

Key Position 3: Contact Point

1.   **Shoulders:** Your shoulders have rotated back roughly halfway toward the original parallel position, with the right shoulder positioned behind the arm and racket. Your upper body is still straight up and down at the waist.

2.   **Hitting arm:** Your palm has pushed the racket forward to the contact. The hitting-arm position remains unchanged, with the elbow in and the wrist laid back. This position creates contact in front of the body and produces natural leverage so your palm can drive the shot.

3.   **Racket:** The racket face is perpendicular to the court and brushes up the back side of the ball. The racket head is positioned in front of the plane of the legs. The shaft of the racket is still parallel to the court.

4.   **Legs:** You have stepped into the shot with the left foot forward so that the tips of the toes are parallel along the edge of a straight line. This represents the target line of the shot. Your weight is forward on the front foot, and your knees have started to uncoil into the ball.

Move from the ready position to the turn and then to the contact. Establish the position physically using the checkpoints. Create the visual image. Close your eyes and visualize the position in detail, making the image and the feeling correspond in your mind.

Work with the key image of the contact if

1. you consistently feel overpowered by the ball,
2. your stroke is "wristy," or
3. your contact with the ball feels rigid or jarring.

Key Position 4: Finish Position

1. **Racket:** Your racket has accelerated to the finish position with the wrist at about eye level. The shaft of the racket is straight up and down with the butt of the racket pointing down at the court. The face of the racket is perpendicular to the left shoulder and the court, ensuring that the swing plane has stayed vertical throughout the foreswing.

2. **Hitting arm:** Your hitting arm is still in the double-bend position, with your elbow about 45 degrees to the court. Your upper arm is parallel to the court surface. Your wrist remains laid back and has not released at impact or through the course of the follow-through.

3. **Shoulders:** Your shoulders and hips have rotated a full 90 degrees until they are again parallel to the net. Your upper body is still straight up and down from the waist. Your left arm is relaxed and has rotated naturally to the left side of the torso.

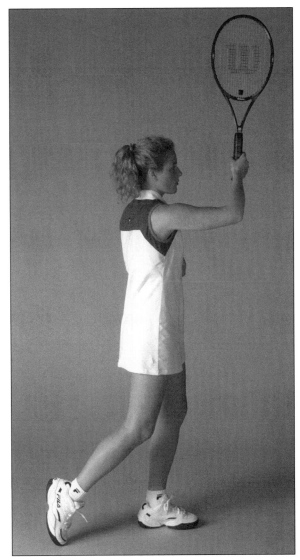

4. **Legs:** Your weight is forward on your left, or front, foot, and you have come up on the toes of your right foot for balance. Your knees remain slightly flexed. The angle of your front foot has naturally opened because of body rotation.

Move through the model from the ready position to the turn, the contact, and the finish. Establish the positions physically. Close your eyes and create a mental image of what the motion looks like and feels like using detail from the checkpoints.

Work with the key image of the finish if

1. you have trouble hitting with depth,

2. your forehand is inconsistent, or

3. you feel you have to muscle the ball or use the wrist to develop ball speed or topspin.

Forehand Key Images

The ultimate purpose of the Visual Tennis training process is to help you develop a forehand that will be reliable under pressure by visualizing a key image of the stroke. The following section outlines a half dozen of the most effective keys for the forehand. Use these to develop the stroke as explained in chapter 9, "Progressive Stroke Development." The key images fuse the physical game with the mental game and provide a method for staying emotionally positive and producing your best strokes under pressure.

Create each key by establishing the physical position and then closing your eyes to create a detailed mental image of how the position looks and feels. Imagine as many details as you can—the color of your racket and strings, or the sound of the ball at contact. Use whatever helps you make the image vivid. You may want to experiment with slight variations of the key images by focusing on one or more of the checkpoints, such as hitting-arm position, wrist position, or the placement of the racket frame in relation to the shoulder.

Besides the finish position key, you should develop two other basic keys for the forehand—the image of the turn and the image of the contact point. These keys will eliminate problems you may have with either aspect of the stroke. Some players may find these keys more effective than the finish position in starting the entire stroke pattern. A highly ranked senior player explained how he used the image of the turn: "Right before I hit my forehand I have an image of the setup in the turn position. When my motion matches the image I know I'm going to make the shot."

Finally, you can experiment with three supplemental forehand images. The first shows you how to key the stroke by visualizing the palm of your hand as the face of the racket. You will find this key particularly effective if you have trouble releasing the wrist at contact, maintaining hitting-arm position, or making contact in front. The last two images are more advanced. The first demonstrates the role of the legs in generating additional power. The second shows you how to vary topspin by hitting up on the ball more sharply at contact. Test these keys when your biomechanics for the basic stroke pattern are solid.

KEY IMAGE 1: FINISH POSITION FROM THE PLAYER'S PERSPECTIVE

The single most powerful key for the forehand is usually some version of the image of the finish position. This is the first key you should test for yourself. If the finish is correct, then the entire stroke pattern will probably be correct. The finish key also eliminates the tendency to overhit on the forehand and maximizes pace and topspin.

The finish image presented here replicates the player's perspective. Most players see themselves in their mind's eye from over the shoulder and slightly behind, but with a 360-degree view. Note that the wrist is at eye level, the hitting arm is in the double-bend position, the shaft of the racket is vertical to the court, and the face of the racket is perpendicular to the left shoulder. Establish the position physically and then create the image. Make the image and the feeling of the position two halves of the same whole in your mind.

KEY IMAGE 2: TURN POSITION FROM THE PLAYER'S PERSPECTIVE

By using this key image of the turn at the start of the stroke, you can quickly correct one of the most fatal technical flaws in stroke production—late preparation. The image shown here is again from the player's perspective, from over the shoulder, the way most players visualize themselves. Note that the shoulders are fully turned. The racket head points straight back to the back fence. The shaft of the racket is parallel to the court, and the face of the racket is perpendicular. The arm is in the double-bend position—elbow in, wrist laid back. Establish the position physically, create the mental image, and imagine how the position feels. As you start the stroke, visualize the key image and use it as a blueprint to establish the position. You should complete the turn immediately, at about the time the ball crosses the net to your side of the court. The full turn should precede your movement to the ball.

KEY IMAGE 3: CONTACT POINT FROM THE PLAYER'S PERSPECTIVE

Focusing on the image of the finish will tend to produce good contact in front of the body automatically. But some players find the image of the contact itself more powerful in executing the stroke. Even if you learn to conform your forehand to the finish image, this key is useful if you find yourself playing an opponent who hits with great pace. You can even combine the contact and finish images into a single key. Instead of a single still image, visualize your racket passing through both positions, or visualize a moving image of your stroke from contact to finish.

Again, this key attempts to re-create the player's perspective. The racket is in front of the front leg. The wrist is laid back so the palm controls the forward motion of the racket. Establish the position physically and then create the mental image with as much detail you can, including how the position feels.

KEY IMAGE 4: VISUALIZING THE PALM AS THE FACE OF THE RACKET

One of the most common errors on the forehand is releasing the wrist at contact, often in a misguided effort to generate topspin. Releasing the wrist detaches the movement of the racket head from the natural course of the swing path and destroys the consistency and power of the classical forehand stroke. To overcome this tendency, visualize yourself hitting the ball with the palm of your hand.

The Visual Tennis grip aligns the palm with the racket head. If your palm pushes through the key positions you will execute a high-quality stroke. This will automatically keep your hitting arm in the classic double-bend position.

Establish the physical position. Now visualize a moving image of your palm hitting the ball as you swing. At the same time visualize how this would feel.

KEY IMAGE 5: USING THE LEGS FOR POWER AND TOPSPIN

By following the basic forehand model, you are already getting leg leverage in your shot. This key maximizes its potential. The thigh muscles, or quadriceps, are the strongest muscles in the body. When you increase knee bend at the completion of the turn and as you step to the ball, you coil the quadriceps as if they were springs. As the racket sweeps forward to the contact, the springs uncoil into the shot automatically. This in turn increases racket-head speed and the brushing action that generates spin. The stroke will still feel effortless and the swing will stay smooth and relaxed, but you will produce noticeably more velocity and ball rotation. Create the physical position by maximizing your knee bend at both the turn and the step to the ball. Then create a mental image of how the position looks and feels in your mind's eye.

KEY IMAGE 6: HITTING UP ON THE BALL FOR TOPSPIN

The forehand swing pattern you have developed will produce topspin automatically. If the racket face is vertical to the court at contact and in its travel to the finish position, the strings will brush up the back side of the ball, causing the ball to rotate over itself naturally. By using this key you can increase the effect. When you face players with more velocity you may find that you need additional spin to control the ball and keep it in the court. Also, when your opponent attacks the net, more spin allows you to dip the ball at your opponent's feet or drop it past him or her more quickly on passing shots. To achieve this, you need only to visualize increasing slightly the steepness of your palm's swing plane. The palm and the racket face should remain vertical but move upward more sharply through the contact. Establish the physical position shown and then visualize hitting upwards as the racket moves forward.

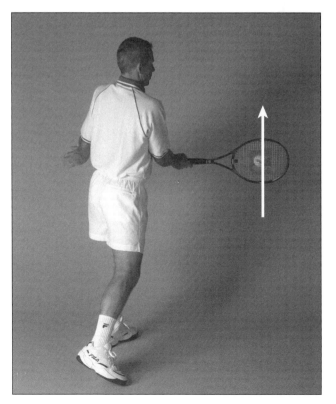

CHAPTER 5

THE BACKHAND

▌t is possible to develop a classical technical style and play winning tennis at any level with either a one-handed or a two-handed backhand. The question you must answer is this: Which stroke will work best in my game?

We can pose this question in two ways. The first is strategic: Which backhand is more effective strategically and better suited to my style of play? The second is practical: Which backhand can I learn and develop most quickly and effectively?

STRATEGIC DIFFERENCES

On the strategy issue, plausible arguments exist on both sides. The one-handed shot is usually associated with serve-and-volley and attacking tennis, and the two-hander with defensive backcourt play. But players with both styles have

© Russ Adams / USTA

Mal Washington's slice backhand models two core Visual Tennis elements. His hitting arm is straight, with the elbow and wrist locked, and the open racket face moves through the line of the shot creating underspin naturally and automatically.

succeeded at all levels of tennis playing a wide range of tactical combinations.

Jimmy Connors helped establish the credibility of the two-handed shot in the modern game, mixing a devastating backcourt-and-return game with well-timed net approaches. Bjorn Borg, probably the greatest defensive player in tennis history, served and volleyed his way to victory in his final Wimbledon championship win over John McEnroe. Ivan Lendl had one of the best one-handed backhands of all time but played predominantly from the backcourt. Boris Becker, another one-handed champion, played serve-and-volley tennis at various stages of his career and baseline tennis at others.

It is safe to say that the one-handed backhand has the advantage in pure serve-and-volley tennis. It isn't a coincidence that virtually every great serve-and-volley player, from Jack Kramer and Billie Jean King to Martina Navratilova, John McEnroe, and Stefan Edberg, has played with one hand. Probably because players learn early to hit the ground stroke and the volley with one hand, they seem to develop into more natural volleyers. Because the one-handed backhand can produce underspin and offers a slightly extended reach, it is superior on low volleys and half volleys. A one-handed player can also take a low ball or short ball, hit a slice approach shot, and follow it to the net.

Although a player can volley well with two hands, a two-handed backhand can be a liability in certain aspects of the transition game from backcourt to net. Players find it difficult to hit low volleys or slices with two hands. Two hands are typically less effective on short balls, low balls, approach shots, and first volleys. In these situations, to get the racket head under the ball, the two-hander has to push the ball up into the air, producing a weaker and more defensive shot. To have a complete game, the two-hander should develop a one-handed slice for these situations. But many players find this difficult because the biomechanics of the shots are so different.

In baseline exchanges, however, two-handers often have a significant advantage. Even the best one-handers tend to generate less pace with their backhand side than with their forehand side. Two-handers often hit as hard or harder off the backhand side, which can prove decisive in matches played from the backcourt. This is why the two-handed backhand has become so dominant in junior tournament tennis.

PRACTICAL DIFFERENCES

Detailed strategic comparisons, though important, are usually less crucial in choosing a pattern than the second consideration: Which backhand can you develop most easily and most rapidly? For junior players, and for many adults as well, the two-handed shot is easier to learn initially. It can quickly become a reliable stroke, sometimes almost immediately. Many junior players do not have the strength to hit the one-handed backhand effectively until the age of 14 or even 16. Players starting at early ages can experience years of frustration trying to develop the one-handed shot.

A ranked junior player who trained at our school put it this way: "Switching from the one-hand backhand to the two-handed was a big key to my success in the juniors." It wasn't that the player's one-handed backhand was dysfunctional—he actually hit it well. But it was clearly a less powerful and less aggressive shot than his forehand. It gave his opponents a point of attack that was the decisive difference in many matches. Using the Visual Tennis pattern he quickly developed a solid two-hander that allowed him to compete with the best players in the section. Over three years he saw his ranking rise from the 30s in his early years to the top 10 in his last year in the juniors.

A one-handed player faces another difficult task. He or she must learn to hit the ball with both slice and topspin in baseline exchanges. Without slice, a one-handed player is almost defenseless against a high ball to the backhand. If a player can master it, the variety the slice offers becomes a strength. But attempting to master two spins simultaneously is impossible for a beginning player or a player trying to reconstruct a one-handed stroke. Most players find it necessary to spend months solidifying either the slice or the topspin drive before adding the other variation. This protracted learning process puts the one-handed player at a substantial and frustrating disadvantage in the interim.

Teaching pros usually consider it counterproductive to teach the one-handed backhand to young juniors. Occasionally, of course, we find the exception—a young player who wants to play attacking or serve-and-volley tennis, who has the extra strength or superior timing to develop a one-handed stroke, or who simply likes the one-handed shot better. Junior players who have the temperament and the volleying ability to play attacking tennis should consider either persevering with one hand or switching from two hands to one when they develop the physical strength. Pete Sampras developed exactly that way when he switched to the one-handed backhand at age 13.

Generally, however, junior players at all levels are better off starting with a two-handed backhand because they will learn the game more rapidly and be able to play at a higher level. Juniors should not spend five or six years trying to play tennis without a backhand. The argument in favor of two hands applies also to many beginning adults, particularly women. Because the two-hander is so easy to learn and because it requires less strength, beginning women pick it up as quickly as they do the forehand. Experienced women players who have struggled for years with ineffective one-handed backhands often have the same experience. After hitting only a few balls with the two-handed shot, many are on the way to solving their backhand problems for life.

Adult men generally have more difficulty learning to hit with two hands. First, the two-handed backhand is technically similar to a left-handed forehand. It therefore requires a player to be at least somewhat ambidextrous so that the left arm and left hand can guide the stroke. Second, it requires greater physical flexibility because the body must rotate more.

The preparation for Andre Agassi's classical two-handed backhand stems from his full body turn. A compact, eliptical loop starts the racket forward to the ball naturally and automatically.

Although rarely a stumbling block for junior or women players, for whatever reason these two requirements usually make it harder for an adult male to develop the shot. For beginning men, the two-handed backhand is often an awkward and stiff shot, unlikely ever to become a flowing, natural stroke. The same can be said for an experienced male player with a weak backhand who decides to experiment with the two-hander. Although men should explore the possibility of hitting with two hands, most will progress more quickly toward a natural stroke if they learn to hit with one hand.

SLICE AND THE BACKHAND

If you choose the one-handed style, you must learn both the topspin drive and the slice. The Visual Tennis models make the development of both variations as simple as possible because their core biomechanical elements are the same. By altering only one variable—the angle and height of the racket head—the Visual Tennis player is able to shift from topspin to slice, as explained below.

Players at the beginning stages will find it very difficult to learn both variations simultaneously. For this reason, beginners should work to solidify one as a basic backhand and add the other later. Which should you develop first? In our oncourt teaching experience, we find that most players are more comfortable learning the drive. But we have found no way to predict which will work best for a given player. We recommend that you start with the model for the topspin drive and see what happens. Some players will have a tendency to come under the ball when trying to learn the drive, that is, they will naturally shift the motion toward the model for the slice. If you or your pro detects the tendency to hit under the ball as you are learning the drive model, you should switch gears and develop the slice model first.

The two-handed player who wants to play at higher levels or play a balanced all-court style should develop the slice backhand after the two-handed drive is solid and consistent.

BACKHAND CORE ELEMENTS

The sequences in this chapter teach the one-handed drive, the one-handed slice, and the two-handed drive from the ground up. Players who want to correct existing strokes can also use the models by comparing their strokes to each of the four key positions. Reviewing a video of your stroke is the best way to determine how your current stroke deviates from the model and which images are critical for you.

As with the forehand, you can hit all the backhand variations shown here off either the front or rear foot in backcourt exchanges. Every player should develop the ability to hit off either foot, as demonstrated in chapter 8, "Court Movement." Success at the higher levels of the game requires it. In developing or correcting your stroke model, however, you will find it easier to develop the key positions by using the basic closed-stance footwork. Later you can learn to hit open stance as you develop your strokes using the Visual Tennis progressive training drills.

Each sequence is broken down into the four key positions, and each key position is broken down further into detailed checkpoints. The key positions are correlated with common technical problems faced by players at all levels. To work on each key position, use the checkpoints to establish the position physically, then create the corresponding mental image. Once you have mastered the appropriate key position, go to chapter 9. Follow the steps to develop the pattern and learn to execute it consistently in competitive play.

Using the sequences for both the two-handed backhand and one-handed backhand, identify the four key positions that you will use to correct or develop the pattern.

The key positions are

1. the ready position,
2. the turn, or preparation,
3. the contact point, and
4. the finish position.

The models themselves follow the same simple principles used for the Visual Tennis forehand. The strokes all include just four core positions. By mastering the physical positions and the corresponding images, you will have a complete framework for developing, executing, and correcting each stroke. Initiate the preparation by a unit turn with the feet and shoulders. To complete the racket positioning, use a short, straight backswing. At the completion of the preparation, set the hitting arm in the hitting position, which positions the racket. This critical hitting-arm position remains unchanged throughout the swing. The hitting-arm position automatically positions the angle of the racket head, which also remains unchanged.

These factors create a compact, minimalist stroke. The strokes all have high finishes with the wrist at eye level, providing a smooth, fluid appearance and effortless feel. In the execution of the model swing, your body and legs generate power and spin naturally and automatically.

As with the forehand, one of the biggest mistakes you can make is initiating the motion with the arm and an independent looping action. The common advice to "get the racket back" is misleading and rarely leads to good preparation, especially on the one-handed backhand. Preparation that starts with a body turn with the shoulders and feet will automatically take the racket back most of the way. The Visual Tennis model simply adds a small, additional straight backswing that establishes the arm and racket in the hitting position with the arm straight and the elbow and wrist locked.

The looping motion *follows* this core preparation. High-speed video studies of top players show that they reestablish this critical straight-arm hitting position at the completion of the loop, well before contact. They maintain this position all the way to the finish. Players who follow the progression here will naturally develop a compact looping motion without having to think about it. The body knows how to change racket direction by using this small loop.

ONE-HANDED BACKHAND STROKE SEQUENCE

VISUAL TENNIS ONE-HANDED BACKHAND MODEL

A common and debilitating problem in hitting the one-handed backhand is the so-called elbow lead, in which the elbow and hand arrive at the contact point before the racket head. Besides preventing the development of a solid basic stroke, this tendency is a main cause of tennis elbow in recreational players. For most players, an elbow lead develops directly from the attempt to establish a circular loop backswing. The circular looping motion begins with a large bend in the elbow. This almost guarantees that the hitting arm will never reach the correct straight-arm hitting position with the arm straight and the elbow and wrist locked. With its straight backswing, the Visual Tennis model immediately places the arm in the correct hitting position. This eliminates the problem of elbow lead before it can start.

Another common technical problem on the one-handed backhand is overrotation of the hips and shoulders during the swing. Here you must recognize a fundamental difference between the one-handed backhand and the forehand. On the forehand, your hitting shoulder must rotate forward to the contact to generate body leverage. On the one-handed backhand, your hitting shoulder moves into the hitting position *at the completion of the turn.* If your

hitting shoulder and your hips rotate forward and sideways away from the contact, you will lose leverage, contact the ball late, and tend to hit with internal motion in the arm.

For this reason, your shoulder position in the Visual Tennis model remains almost completely perpendicular to the direction of the shot throughout the swing. To keep this sideways position your left arm opposes, or moves back away from, the shot at the start of the foreswing. Following this model some players will naturally develop some shoulder and hip rotation. Others will be able to keep almost fully perpendicular, as Stan Smith demonstrates so beautifully in the Sybervision video.

Not every player has the strength to hit from this fully perpendicular position. Even some top players have as much as 45 degrees of hip and shoulder rotation. Some students who observe this make a conscious effort to rotate through the shot. Unfortunately, this leads to overrotation and a loss of both power and control—particularly disastrous when paired with a loop backswing. We have all seen players with large looping swings rotate their bodies wildly through the one-handed shot. For all that effort, they generate almost no ball velocity or spin.

By following the model above and keying the sideways shoulder position, you will maximize your leverage. Any rotation that occurs will happen naturally in the course of the swing.

ONE-HANDED BACKHAND KEY POSITIONS

Key Position 1: Ready Position

1. **Shoulders:** Your shoulders face the net in the ready position. Your upper body is straight up and down from the waist. Your bend is in the knees, not the waist.

2. **Hitting arm:** Your hitting arm is positioned so that the elbows tuck in toward the waist, just as it does for the forehand. Wait with the forehand grip.

3. **Racket:** The racket is slightly below waist level and points directly at the net. The face of the racket is perpendicular to the court surface.

4. **Legs:** Your legs are slightly wider than shoulder-width. Your knees are flexed, and your weight is slightly forward on the balls of your feet.

Close your eyes. Visualize yourself with detail in the correct ready position. Notice how the position feels. Make the image and the feeling correspond in your mind.

Work with the key image of the ready position if

1. you feel slow getting the motion started,
2. you feel off balance when hitting the stroke, or
3. you have problems recovering for the next shot.

Key Position 2: Turn Position

1. **Shoulders:** Your shoulders have rotated 90 degrees, from parallel to the net to perpendicular to the net. Your right shoulder is pointing directly at the net, and your head is turned to follow the oncoming ball. Your shoulder turn has completed most of the racket preparation.

2. **Hitting arm:** Your preparation is completed with a short, straight backswing. Your hitting arm should be straight, already in the hitting position. Your racket hand should be in line with the middle of your back leg, which naturally positions the racket below waist level.

3. **Racket:** Through the turn and the straight backswing, the racket has traveled straight back until it is pointing at the back fence. The shaft of the racket is horizontal, or parallel, to the court. The butt of the racket is visible to your opponent. The face of the racket is still perpendicular to the court.

4. **Legs:** You have initiated the turn with a pivot or a sideways step with the left foot so it is pointing to the side fence. Your weight is on your left foot, and you use the toes of your right foot for balance. Your knees are still flexed.

Move from the ready position to the turn. Establish the position physically using the checkpoints and then create the mental image. Imagine with detail how the position looks and feels.

Work with the key position of the turn if

1. your preparation is consistently late or you feel rushed by the ball,

2. you tend to lead the shot with your elbow, or

3. you have trouble hitting topspin.

ONE-HANDED BACKHAND KEY POSITIONS

Key Position 3: Contact Point

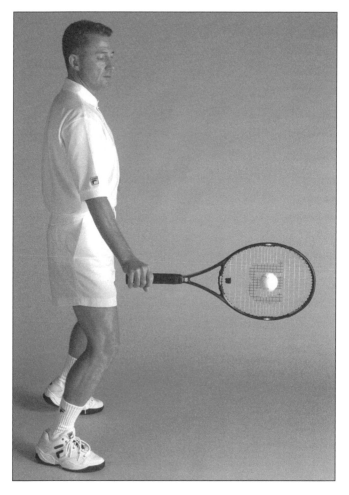

1. **Shoulders:** The hitting arm and racket have swung foreward to the contact point from the shoulder, like the action of a gate hinge. Keep your shoulders and hips sideways so they do not rotate or rotate only slightly staying at about 90 degrees to the net. Your upper body is straight up and down from the waist.

2. **Hitting arm:** Your hitting arm is still completely straight, with the wrist locked. This position creates early contact and ensures full transfer of body leverage into the ball.

3. **Racket:** The racket face has moved forward and slightly upward to the ball. The face is still vertical, or perpendicular, to the court. This ensures that the racket will brush the back of the ball automatically, creating topspin.

4. **Legs:** You have stepped forward with your right foot to the ball so that your toes are parallel, along the edge of a straight line. This line is parallel to the target line of the shot. Your weight is forward on the right foot, and your knees have started to uncoil.

Move from the ready position through the turn to the contact point. Establish the position physically using the checkpoints and then create the mental image. Imagine with detail how the position looks and feels.

Work with the key position of the contact if

1. you consistently feel overpowered by the ball, or
2. your stroke is "wristy" or your elbow is ahead of the racket at contact.

Key Position 4: Finish Position

1. **Racket:** The racket has accelerated upward to the finish position. Your wrist is at eye level. The shaft of the racket is straight up and down, with the butt pointing straight down at the court. The racket has swung 30 to 45 degrees past perpendicular to the net.

2. **Hitting arm:** Your arm is still straight, as it has been throughout the motion, with the elbow and wrist locked. The wrist has not released at impact or through the course of the follow-through.

3. **Shoulders:** Your hips and shoulders have stayed predominantly sideways, or perpendicular, to the net, with no conscious effort to rotate them through the shot. Your upper body remains straight up and down from the waist. Your back arm has moved back away from the direction of the shot, keeping the torso sideways.

4. **Legs:** Your weight is fully forward on the right, or front, foot. You have come up on the toes of your left, rear, foot for balance. Your knees have uncoiled into the ball but remain slightly flexed.

Move from the ready position through the turn to the contact point and the finish position. Establish the position physically using the checkpoints and then create the mental image. Notice how the position feels and make the image and the feeling correspond in your mind.

Work with the key position of the finish if

1. you have trouble hitting with depth,
2. your backhand is inconsistent, or
3. you feel you have to muscle the ball or use wrist to develop ball speed or topspin.

One-Handed Topspin Backhand Key Images

The crucial step in developing a reliable backhand is creating a personal system of stroke keys. A key is a single element of the stroke pattern that you use to activate the entire stroke in actual play. In the split second before hitting the shot you visualize the key. By holding this mental image in mind, you trigger the correct execution of the entire stroke pattern. For the one-handed topspin backhand, an active key could be the image of any of the four still frames or an image of any checkpoint.

As with the forehand, the single most effective key is usually an image of the finish position. Any stroke that finishes correctly was probably correct on its way to the finish. You may also want to experiment with slight variations of the image. Focus, for example, on one of the checkpoints, such as keeping the wrist at eye level or maintaining a straight hitting arm. The image is presented from the player's perspective, which is how most players will see the key inside the mind's eye.

Besides the finish, this section includes two other basic key images that most players find effective. These are images for the contact point and the turn, both seen from the player's perspective. If you are having difficulty with late contact or with preparation of the racket, you should work with these keys. Some players prefer these images over the image of the finish. Create the key images by using the process described earlier.

There are two additional key images. The first key helps to increase the knee bend and expand the role of the legs in the shot. This key will help you add pace and spin once your basic biomechanics are solid. The second of these focuses on maintaining the straight hitting-arm position throughout the swing. This is a critical element in the one-handed backhand. If you have struggled with an elbow lead in your backhand, this image can eliminate it, sometimes instantaneously.

After you have established the key images presented here, go to "Progressive Stroke Development," chapter 9, and work through the drills and progressions for incorporating the keys into play.

KEY IMAGE 1: FINISH POSITION FROM THE PLAYER'S PERSPECTIVE

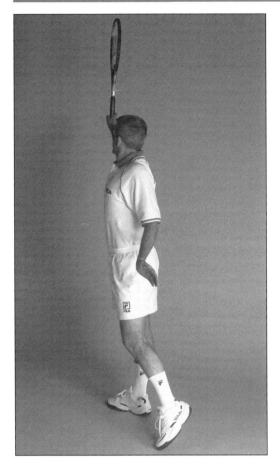

The image of the finish position is usually the most powerful single key for the backhand because the entire stroke pattern must be correct to produce a correct finish. Students often ask why follow-through is so important if the ball is already off the strings at the contact point.

The answer is that the finish position determines how the racket is moving at the contact point, and thus the nature of the hit. The racket face must be accelerating upward and outward toward the finish position to create power and spin at contact. Note that the racket shaft is vertical, the arm is straight with the wrist at eye level, and the swing has gone slightly past perpendicular to the net. Establish the position physically and create the mental image. Imagine how the position looks and especially how it feels.

KEY IMAGE 2: TURN POSITION FROM THE PLAYER'S PERSPECTIVE

If you have problems with incomplete or late preparation, you can overcome them by using this key image. Again, the key is from the player's perspective, which is how most of us see ourselves in our mind's eye. Note several key elements. Your shoulders are fully turned. Your racket is all the way back with the arm straight and your racket hand in the middle of the back leg. The racket face is *vertical* to the court. Establish the physical position and create the mental image. Imagine how it looks and feels. You should visualize the image as your opponent strikes the ball. Remember the turn move precedes the movement to the ball. Your goal should be to complete the turn *before* the ball reaches your side of the court, or at the latest, before the bounce in higher speed exchanges.

KEY IMAGE 3: CONTACT POINT FROM THE PLAYER'S PERSPECTIVE

This image creates the key for the contact point from the player's perspective. Although a correct finish position will usually result in correct contact, many players find it effective to focus on the image of the contact point itself, particularly in fast exchanges. When you make contact well in front of your front leg, you increase body leverage on the ball. Your hitting arm is straight, and the racket is vertical to the court. From this viewpoint you can also see how continuing the swing outward and upward will result in the racket face brushing the ball, creating topspin. Establish the physical position and create the mental image, including how the position feels.

KEY IMAGE 4: USING THE LEGS FOR POWER AND TOPSPIN

If you watch great players such as Pete Sampras, Boris Becker, or Ivan Lendl hit one-handed topspin drives, you may have been struck by the tremendous leverage they generate from their legs. Occasionally, you'll see so much bend that the back knee touches the court. Few players have the strength and flexibility to go down this far, but every player, after developing a reliable basic stroke pattern, should try to maximize knee bend. By going down as far as you can at both the turn and the step to the ball, you increase the uncoiling action of the legs into the ball at contact. This adds racket-head speed and increases the natural brushing action of the strings on the ball. The result is significant additional ball velocity and topspin. This is particularly important when hitting passing shots. Establish the position physically and create the mental image of how the position looks and feels.

KEY IMAGE 5: MAINTAINING A STRAIGHT HITTING-ARM POSITION

Set up the straight hitting-arm position at the completion of the turn. By doing this you eliminate the possibility of developing of an elbow lead and ensure that you achieve maximum body leverage on the ball. With your arm in the straight position at the completion of the preparation, you need only to maintain the correct alignment at the contact point and at the finish position. Establish each of the three positions shown physically and create the mental images, including the feeling of the positions. The key can be an image of the arm at any of the three positions or a mini-movie of the entire motion.

ONE-HANDED SLICE BACKHAND STROKE SEQUENCE

VISUAL TENNIS ONE-HANDED SLICE BACKHAND MODEL

The one-handed slice backhand is hit with the same classical grip as the topspin shot. Again, you should shift your grip immediately at the start of the turn. Hit this shot as you do the topspin version, with the arm straight and the wrist locked. This hitting-arm position never changes during the swing. Note that your right, or hitting, shoulder is already in front at the completion of the turn. The arm and racket are like a one-piece gate swinging on the hinge of the shoulder. The contact is well in front of your front leg. Again, you will use far less body rotation than on the forehand. In the model, the torso remains sideways, or perpendicular, to the net. With the slice, the torso may open naturally as much or even more than on the drive, but this rotation is not part of the model.

The two variations of the one-handed backhand differ in two important ways. First, to achieve underspin rather than topspin, hit the slice backhand with the racket face *slightly open* rather than perpendicular to the court. Second, instead of starting below the ball, make the slice backswing at the level of the ball or slightly above. If the ball

is high or low, raise or lower the racket accordingly. From this position, the racket face comes through the ball on a straight line, allowing the racket head to impart natural slice.

To create slice, the racket must move through the contact point with the face slightly open, about 30 to 45 degrees to the court surface. Visualize the ball as an orange and the face of the racket as a knife. Use the knife to slice off the bottom diagonal third of the ball. The strings will bite as they slide under the ball, causing the ball to rotate backward under itself with underspin, or slice.

Unlike a topspin ground stroke, the slice is not hit with a vertical swing plane. As you would with a topspin forehand or backhand, set the angle of the racket face to the court by the completion of the turn and maintain that angle throughout the swing. This gives the shot a technical simplicity characteristic of the classical style. Once you set the face of the racket properly, you will generate underspin automatically during the swing. Early contact ensures that your body weight transfers naturally into the shot. As with the topspin backhand, the uncoiling of your legs will generate additional racket-head speed, spin, and shot velocity.

KEY IMAGE 1: ANGLE OF THE RACKET FACE

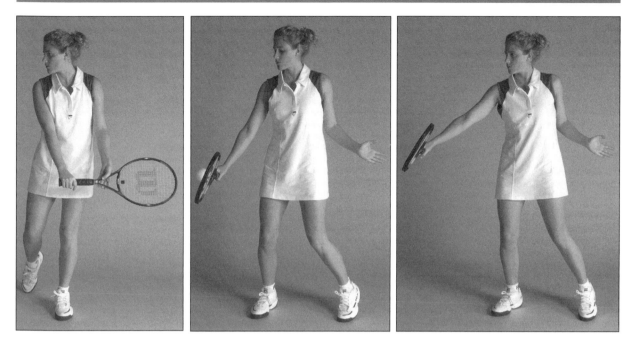

The key to executing the slice backhand is setting the racket face correctly at the completion of the turn. Set the face open at about 30 to 45 degrees to the court. The level of the racket head should be at the level of the ball or slightly higher. Once you set the angle correctly, it remains unchanged throughout the stroke, at the contact point, and at the start of the follow-through. Apart from this difference, the biomechanics of the slice swing pattern are virtually identical to the topspin variation. Your arm is straight throughout the swing, the back arm opposes helping to keep the body sideways, and the contact point itself is well in front of your front leg.

Note also that the racket face moves outward along the line of the shot and only then starts upward to the finish. It is common for players to swing sharply downward in an attempt to create slice. But this radical chopping motion will result in late contact, loss of body leverage and pace, and a tendency for the ball to float. Instead, the racket face moves through the ball. This follows the model of the great Ken Rosewall. The slice is the automatic consequence of this swing plane.

Use the images as the basis for your keys on the slice backhand. Your key can be any of the three individual frames or a mini-movie of the entire motion. You should also experiment with the keys for keeping your arm straight and increasing your knee bend as described in the section on the topspin backhand.

VISUAL TENNIS TWO-HANDED BACKHAND MODEL

As with the one-handed backhand models, the two-handed backhand teaching progression begins with the photo sequence of the entire stroke. The sequence is the blueprint you will use to create your swing, or correct existing errors by comparing your current stroke to the model. The four key positions and the corresponding checkpoints are then identified. When you have worked through the key positions and the key images that follow, go to chapter 9 and follow the drills and exercises for mastering the pattern and learning to execute the stroke under competitive pressure.

For the two-handed player, the Visual Tennis model presented here embodies the core elements of the strokes of some of the greatest two-handed players in tennis history—Chris Evert, Jimmy Connors, Michael Chang, Andre Agassi, and Martina Hingis. Despite differences in temperament, tactical style, and seeming variation in their strokes, video analysis shows that these players and all good classical two-handers approximate the four key positions of the Visual Tennis model. To develop the stroke, you should match the core positions rather than the idiosyncrasies of individual players. Still-frame analysis shows that a player like Chang, with a loop in his backswing and a radical wrap at the finish of his stroke, passes through the same critical positions as a player with a seemingly more compact stroke like Agassi.

The positions include a unit turn that completes the bulk of the racket preparation, the classical two-handed hitting-arm position, and a finish position at eye level with the plane of the racket perpendicular to the court. The biomechanics of the classical two-hander presented here are similar to those used to hit a forehand with the opposite hand. The top, or opposite, hand grasps the racket with a forehand grip. (Refer to chapter 3 for an explanation of grips.) You should set up with a hitting-arm position identical to the one you used for the forehand. Drive the shot with the palm of this hand so that your hips and shoulders rotate 90 degrees through the shot. The finish position is almost identical to the classical forehand—your wrist is at eye level and the plane of the racket is perpendicular with the opposite shoulder.

TWO-HANDED BACKHAND STROKE SEQUENCE

The two-handed shot itself can be hit well with two forehand grips. By shifting the bottom hand to the one-handed backhand grip, however, you can later develop a one-handed slice. The bottom hand adds extra support and stability but plays a secondary role. Note the difference between this and other versions of the "two-hander," such as that of Bjorn Borg, in which the player lets go early in the swing and uses the second hand primarily to push the racket to the contact. This push does not extend to the finish, so the shot relies to a much greater degree on the front arm.

The stroke sequence above demonstrates the core elements shared by all great two-handed backhands. The compact preparation is completed primarily by the shoulder turn. The back left hitting arm drives the shot, and remains in the classical, double-bend position, with no wrist release all the way through the finish.

You can use the progression to develop the entire stroke, or use one or more of the key positions to correct your own specific problems. By developing the physical and mental models of the simple key positions, you create the building blocks for your own great classical backhand and the mental toughness to execute it under pressure.

Two-Handed Backhand Key Positions

The following section presents the four key positions for mastering the building blocks of the Visual Tennis two-handed backhand. Use the four numbered checkpoints to create the physical model for each position and a corresponding kinesthetic image of how each position looks and feels inside your mind's eye. This should be done without the ball. Work until you can execute the swing pattern naturally and automatically without the ball, passing accurately through each of the key positions. Take the time at the start of your work to become comfortable with the checkpoints and you will find that you will develop the stroke rapidly and effortlessly on the court.

TWO-HANDED BACKHAND KEY POSITIONS

Key Position 1: Ready Position

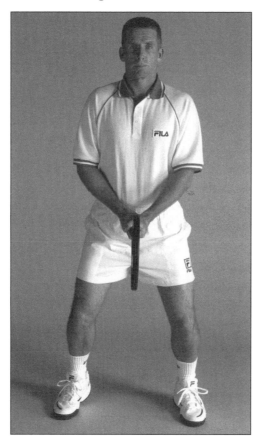

1. **Shoulders:** Your shoulders face the net in the ready position. Your upper body is straight up and down from the waist. Your bend is in the knees, not the waist.

2. **Hitting arm:** The hitting arm is positioned so that the elbows tuck in toward the waist. The hands are together with two forehand grips.

3. **Racket:** The racket is slightly below waist level, pointing directly at the net. The face of the racket is perpendicular to the court surface.

4. **Legs:** The legs are slightly wider than shoulder width. Your knees are flexed, and your weight is slightly forward on the balls of your feet.

Close your eyes and visualize yourself with detail in the correct ready position. Notice how the position feels. Make the image andthe feeling correspond in your mind.

Work with the key position of the ready position if

1. you feel slow getting the motion started,

2. you feel off balance when hitting the stroke, or

3. you have problems recovering for the next shot.

Key Position 2: Turn Position

1. **Shoulders:** Your shoulders have rotated 90 degrees and are now perpendicular to the net. Your right shoulder is pointing directly at the net, and your head is turned to follow the oncoming ball.

2. **Hitting arm:** Your back, or left, hitting arm is in the double-bend position, with your elbow in toward the waist and your wrist laid back. You have shifted to the backhand grip with your right hand. At the completion of the turn, your right hand is in line with the middle of your back leg.

3. **Racket:** Your racket has traveled straight back along a line and points at the back fence. The shaft of the racket is parallel to the court surface. The butt of the racket is visible to your opponent. The face of the racket is perpendicular to the court.

4. **Legs:** Both feet have pivoted or stepped sideways and are pointing to the side fence. Your weight is on the left, or pivot, foot. You use the toes of your right foot for balance. Your knees are still flexed.

Move from the ready position to the turn. Establish the position using the checkpoints and then create the mental image. Notice how the position feels and make the image and the feeling correspond in your mind.

Work with the key position of the turn if

1. your preparation is consistently late,
2. your shot lacks power, or
3. you have trouble hitting topspin.

TWO-HANDED BACKHAND KEY POSITIONS

Key Position 3: Contact Point

1. **Shoulders:** Your shoulders have rotated back about halfway to their original position. Your back shoulder is solidly behind the arm and racket, driving the shot through with body rotation. Your upper body is still straight up and down from the waist.

2. **Hitting arm:** Your hitting arm is still in the classical hitting-arm position, with the elbow bent and the wrist laid back. The palm of your hand has pushed the racket forward to the contact point, ensuring the proper sequence of body rotation. This position creates early contact and full transfer of body leverage.

3. **Racket:** The face has moved slightly upward to contact, creating the brushing effect for topspin. The face of the racket is perpendicular to the court, and the contact point is in front of the plane of your front leg. The shaft of the racket is parallel to the court surface.

4. **Legs:** You have stepped forward with your right foot so your toes are parallel along the edge of a straight line. This line is parallel to the target line of the shot. Your weight is fully forward on the right foot, and your knees have started to uncoil into the ball.

Move from the ready position through the turn to the contact point. Establish the position physically using the checkpoints and then create the mental image. Notice how the position feels. Make the image and the feeling correspond in your mind.

Work with the key position of the contact if

1. you consistently feel overpowered by the ball,
2. your stroke is "wristy," or
3. contact with the ball feels rigid or jarring.

Key Position 4: Finish Position

1. **Racket:** The racket has moved upward to the finish position. Your left wrist is at about eye level. The shaft of the racket is straight up and down, with the butt pointing directly down at the court. The edges of the frame are perpendicular to your right shoulder and to the net.

2. **Hitting arm:** Your left arm finishes in the double-bend position. Your elbow is bent, with the forearm about 45 degrees from horizontal with the court. Your upper arm is parallel to the court surface. Your wrist has not released and remains laid back. Your *right* arm has collapsed at the elbow.

3. **Shoulders:** Your shoulders have rotated back fully parallel to the net, as they were in the ready position. They have rotated a full 90 degrees through the course of the shot, providing power naturally and automatically.

4. **Legs:** Your weight is fully forward on the right, or front, foot. You have come up on the toes of your rear foot for balance. The toes of your front foot have naturally opened through the course of your body rotation. Your knees have uncoiled into the ball but remain slightly bent.

Move from the ready position to the turn, contact, and finish. Establish the position physically using the checkpoints and then create the mental image. Notice how the position feels. Make the image and the feeling correspond in your mind.

Work with the key position of the finish if

1. you have trouble hitting with depth,

2. your backhand is inconsistent, or

3. you feel you have to muscle the ball or use wrist to develop ball speed or topspin.

Two-Handed Backhand Key Images

The ultimate purpose of the Visual Tennis training process is to help you develop strokes that will be reliable under pressure, by visualizing key images during actual play. The following section outlines five of the most effective keys for the two-handed backhand that you can use to develop the stroke, as explained in chapter 9. The key images fuse the physical and the mental game and provide a method for staying emotionally positive and producing your best strokes in competition.

Create each key by establishing the physical position and then closing your eyes and creating a detailed mental image of how the position looks and feels. Imagine the details—the color of your racket and strings, the sound of the ball at contact, whatever will make the image vivid. Practice visualizing the key and then swinging out over the image with your eyes closed. Now work through the progressive levels described in chapter 9. You may want to experiment with slight variations of the keys presented here by focusing on one or more of the checkpoints, such as hitting-arm position, wrist position, or the edge of the racket frame in relation to the shoulder.

The first key image is the finish position, presented from the perspective of how most players will naturally visualize the image inside their minds. As with the other ground strokes, this is usually the most effective key. Consequently, most players should experiment with it first. Two other basic keys are the image of the turn and the image of the contact point, also presented from the player's perspective. If you have difficulty with either of these aspects of the stroke, focus on these keys. Some players may find these keys more effective than the finish position key in activating the entire stroke pattern.

Finally, two supplemental image keys may prove effective for you. The first demonstrates the role of the legs in generating additional power. The second key shows you how to vary the amount of topspin by hitting up on the ball more sharply at contact.

KEY IMAGE 1: FINISH POSITION FROM THE PLAYER'S PERSPECTIVE

The finish position for the two-handed backhand is the most basic, and usually the most effective key. If you produce a correct finish, the stroke leading up to the finish must be correct as well. If you visualize yourself in your mind's eye, you probably will see yourself from a perspective similar to the key shown. Note that your left wrist is at about eye level, your arm is still in the double-bend position, and the racket is straight up and down. The front edge of the racket is perpendicular to the net, and the rear edge is perpendicular to your right shoulder. The shoulders and hips have rotated through the shot until they are parallel with the net.

KEY IMAGE 2: TURN POSITION FROM THE PLAYER'S PERSPECTIVE

Unless your turn is correct on the two-handed backhand, as with any ground stroke you will find it impossible to execute a solid stroke. If you are having problems with your preparation, you should work intensively with this key. Again, this key is shown from the player's perspective. Note that your hitting arm is in double-bend position with the left elbow into the waist, the tip of the racket is pointing toward the back fence, and the face of the racket is perpendicular to the court. The racket is below waist level. Establish the position physically and create the mental image. You should complete the turn motion before any court movement. Your goal should be to finish the turn before the opponent's ball reaches your side of the net, or at the latest, before the bounce.

KEY IMAGE 3: CONTACT POINT FROM THE PLAYER'S PERSPECTIVE

Keying the image of the finish will tend to produce good contact in front of the body automatically. But some players find the image of the contact itself more powerful in executing the stroke. Even if you learn to key your backhand to the finish image, this key is useful if you find yourself playing an opponent who hits with great pace. You can also combine the contact and finish images into a single key. Instead of a single still image, visualize your racket passing through both positions or visualize a moving image of your stroke from contact to finish.

Again, the key attempts to re-create the player's perspective. The racket is in front of your front leg, and your hitting arm is in the double-bend position. Create the position physically and then create the mental image with detail.

KEY IMAGE 4: USING THE LEGS FOR POWER AND SPIN

One characteristic of all great two-handed players is their use of the legs to execute the stroke. Andre Agassi, Michael Chang, Martina Hingis, Jimmy Connors, Chris Evert, Bjorn Borg—all generate the pace of their backhand drives in part from the legs up. By maximizing your knee bend, you guarantee that your legs will release into the shot. As your legs uncoil, they generate additional racket-head speed and body leverage. This translates into power and topspin. Effective use of the legs can add velocity that transforms a solid, consistent two-handed shot into a weapon. At the completion of the turn, increase the coiling in your back leg and do the same at the step to the ball. Establish the position physically and create the mental image of how the position looks and feels in your mind's eye.

KEY IMAGE 5: INCREASING TOPSPIN

Many players release their wrists through the stroke, believing they can generate more power or spin. Releasing the wrists detaches the movement of the racket head from the natural course of the swing path and destroys the consistency and power of the stroke. If the palm pushes the motion through the key positions, the stroke execution will be of extremely high quality. By increasing the upward brushing action of the palm as the racket moves across the back of the ball, you can increase the amount of topspin. Establish the physical position shown above. Create an internal mental image of how the key looks and feels inside your mind's eye.

CHAPTER 6

PLAYING THE NET

In one way the volley, because it has the shortest swing pattern, is the simplest of all basic strokes. A good technical volley has no real backswing and little follow-through. Most players, however, find the volley the most difficult stroke to hit successfully in matches. The reason is that the player at the net is closer to the opponent, about half as far away compared to the backcourt. So the net player has about half the time to react to the ball and execute the stroke. This requires faster hand-eye coordination, quicker footwork, and better balance.

Playing effective serve-and volley tennis can be the most dominating, quickest, and possibly most satisfying way to win matches. Pure serve-and-volley players, however, are probably born, not made. Only two great players in the last two decades, John McEnroe and Martina Navratilova, have been pure attacking players. With ever increasing ball speeds in pro tennis, playing winning serve-and-volley points has become more difficult. Conventional wisdom has always held that the server should reach the service line for the first volley. Video analysis shows that on a hard court even Pete Sampras can take only two steps into the court before making his split step. This places him about halfway between the baseline and the service line. From this position, the first volley is a difficult shot to hit consistently.

Although the ball speed is much reduced, playing serve-and-volley tennis in recreational tennis is also difficult. Because of the reduced reaction times and the difficulty of key shots such as the first volley, few players can successfully make serve and volley their primary match strategy. But most players, especially those who are not naturally confident volleyers, do not use the net enough. Many players are terrified of the net because the play is so much faster. By using the Visual Tennis approach, however, you can learn to play the net competently and aggressively. This includes developing an effective and reliable overhead.

Following the volley progressions you will develop the ability to play the net in doubles and incorporate net play into effective singles strategy. In singles, playing the all-court game is critical to competing well. This means getting ahead in backcourt rallies, forcing short balls and coming in, attacking the second serve, and playing serve-and volley points against certain opponents.

One of the best descriptions of a volley is that it is like setting up a mirror in front of a laser beam. The goal is to redirect the beam at an angle that produces superior ball placement. At the net, because you are about half as far away from your opponent, the angles between the players are much sharper. A ball volleyed to the sideline from the net will force a player on the baseline much wider out of the court than a ground stroke hit to the same spot. The radical angles that are available at the net are the key to producing winning placements. To hit a winning volley you simply take advantage of the superior geometry of your position in redirecting your opponent's shots.

A key note: the ability to focus on the ball is the critical first element in developing the volley. Although many players get away with poor ball focus in the backcourt, watching the ball and reacting as the opponent makes a shot are prerequisites at the net. Keying on the flight of the ball as it leaves the opponent's racket will give you the time to develop the Visual Tennis volley patterns.

COMPARING VOLLEYS TO GROUND STROKES

With its reduced backswing and abbreviated finish, a good volley has much less technical motion than a ground stroke or a serve. The volley differs from other basic shots in another crucial aspect: it requires an earlier contact point. In learning to volley, most players replicate the feeling and timing of their ground strokes by contacting the ball at the front edge of the body. But the foreswing on the volley should *start* at about the point where the racket contacts the ball on a ground stroke, with the contact at least a foot further in front. Because they

© Steve Margheim

The classical volley starts its swing near the contact point for a ground stroke—at the front edge of the body. Pete Sampras keeps his forearm parallel to the court and the racket at about 45 degrees.

do not develop the feeling of effortless power that comes from this earlier contact, many players take the volley late and consistently overswing or muscle the ball.

In the Visual Tennis system, you complete the preparation for the volley with a step or pivot and a shoulder turn that includes no independent backswing. The racket moves forward from this turn position to the contact point. In professional tennis, the most aggressive and effective volleyers—Sampras, McEnroe, and Navratilova—make the volley look easy. By taking the ball farther in front than other players, these champions create superior body leverage. This body leverage produces natural power with minimal effort. Taking the ball early at the net allows you to hit a crisp winning volley rather than a placement that your opponent can reach and return.

THE QUESTION OF GRIPS

The simplicity and effectiveness of the Visual Tennis models allow you to develop solid technical volleys and the confidence to use them in match play. But before turning to the stroke patterns, we must answer two important questions. The first is whether you should change grips at the net.

Probably no absolute answer exists in the discussion of changing grips. Jack Kramer, who virtually invented the serve-and-volley game, changed grips. But Rod Laver and John McEnroe, the two most devastating attacking players to follow Kramer, hit all their volleys with the same continental grip. Martina Navratilova used the single grip, as does Pete Sampras. With the increased shot velocity in the modern era, it is preferable, at higher levels of play, to hit all volleys without grip changes.

But for most beginners, and even for some experienced players, this technique can be difficult to master. The basic volley models presented here use the same eastern grips as the ground strokes. When first learning the volley motions, you should learn to hit volleys flat, without underspin, focusing on biomechanics and establishing solid contact. This will happen naturally using the groundstroke grips.

After you develop solid basic mechanics of the volley, you can experiment with the continental grip, which is halfway between the classical forehand and backhand. If you are unsure about the continental grip or are developing it for the first time, you should refer to the chapter on Visual Tennis grips. Besides eliminating the time and movement required for the grip shift, using the single volley grip makes it easier to hit the ball with underspin, particularly on the forehand side. Underspin, a necessity on low volleys, angled placements, and touch volleys, gives you more control of the ball. With the eastern forehand grip you must move the racket face sharply under the ball to produce underspin.

With the continental grip, however, you can produce underspin on the forehand while still hitting through the ball on the line of the shot. The change of grip alters the angle of the racket face so that it slides under the ball automatically. The same is true to a lesser extent on the backhand volley, which also requires a downward motion in the swing when hit with the eastern backhand grip. Some players will take quite rapidly to the slice volley with the continental grip. Others, even players at higher competitive levels, are never able to hit the shot naturally and are better off sticking with the grip switch at the net.

Like the ground-stroke models, the volleys use the simplest possible preparation, without any loop or backswing. In the words of a top pro coach, "The shoulder turn *is* the backswing." Following the Visual Tennis models, you will automatically develop a small compact loop to change the direction of the racket head. A conscious attempt to add a loop to volley preparation usually leads to disastrous results.

HOW MANY HANDS?

The second key question in learning the volley is whether two-handed backhanders should volley with one hand or two. Here the answer is more clear cut—most two-handed ground strokers should also learn the two-handed volley. Jimmy Connors, among others, has shown that it is possible to volley well with two hands. If we look to tennis history we can see that Frew McMillian, the great South African doubles players, volleyed with two hands on *both* sides. Mary Pierce is an example of a top modern player with an extremely effective two-handed backhand volley.

Many women or younger junior players find it almost impossible to learn to volley competently with one hand. The one-handed volley takes more strength than the two-handed volley, and the biomechanics of the two styles are completely opposed. A player who has mastered the backhand ground stroke with two hands can quickly and naturally draw on this feeling in developing a two-handed volley. He or she has already developed the biomechanics of hitting with the left arm and shoulder, which is the core movement in the two-handed volley.

The two-handed volley will produce excellent results in both an all-court singles game and a doubles game. For players below the highest levels, continuity on the biomechanics of the backhand in the backcourt and at the net is the best approach. Players with strong two-handed backhands who nevertheless want to play more attacking tennis can always experiment with the one-handed volley.

VOLLEY CORE ELEMENTS

As with the ground strokes, the volley models presented here are based on simple hitting-arm positions. At the completion of the turn, you set the arm and racket in the hitting position. This position remains unchanged through the course of the volley. Use the larger muscle groups in the torso to move the arm and racket through the motion. The models use no internal arm motion. The model for the overhead is equally compact, based on an immediate body turn and racket preparation before any movement to the ball.

The role of the shoulders and the hitting arm in the volley has been generally misunderstood in instructional theory. The forehand volley is often described as a punching motion, similar to a jab in boxing. This implies that the arm straightens out to full extension at the hit. But if you observe the top volleyers in the history of the game—John McEnroe, Pete Sampras, Martina Navratilova, Stefan Edberg, Boris Becker—you will see that the genesis of the motion forward to the ball on the forehand volley lies in the rotation of the shoulders and a push with the palm. Like the forehand groundstroke, the hitting arm is set up in a double-bend position, with the elbow in and the wrist laid back at the turn. Rather than straightening out, this hitting-arm position remains basically unchanged through the course of the shot.

The same is true of the two-handed volley. The back-arm is in a double-bend hitting position that is virtually identical to the forehand—the elbow is in and the wrist laid back. Like the two-handed ground stroke, the core movement is a unitary body rotation.

For the one-handed backhand volley the basic technical concept is similar. Again, you set up a fixed hitting-arm position at the completion of the turn. The racket and hitting-arm position resembles an open "U" shape. Your forearm is parallel to the court surface, and you set your upper arm and racket at about a 45-degree angle. Once you set up this position at the completion of the turn, it remains unchanged throughout the stroke. The difference compared to the forehand and two-handed backhand volley is that with one-hand the shoulders stay sideways and there is minimal or no torso rotation. Instead the deltoids and other upper-body muscle groups move the arm and racket to the ball. Like the forehand, however, they are moving as a unit, with the hitting arm position staying unchanged.

Because of the speed of exchanges at the net, simplicity is critical. The volley models here are all built using this combination of unit turns, set hitting-arm positions, and early contact points. By following the models players at any level can develop the ability to volley solidly and aggressively with economy of motion and effort.

To learn to hit or to improve your volleys, we will use the same photo sequence progressions we used for the ground strokes. The sequences will serve as the blueprint for developing your swing pattern or making corrections to an existing stroke. The sequences identify the four key positions that are the building blocks of the models.
These four key positions are

1. the ready position,
2. the turn,
3. the contact point, and
4. the finish position.

As with the ground strokes, you can see that if the motion is correct at each of the key positions, it will be correct throughout the whole pattern. This is particularly true on the volleys because the motions are so compact that little can go wrong between the key positions. The application of each key position to common technical problems is also explained. Experienced players who want to correct technical errors or improve their volleys should begin by comparing their stroke to the model by using video.

In the following section, you will learn the four key positions individually, through a series of simple checkpoints, and how to put them together into a complete swing pattern. This reduces learning or correcting the stroke to a *maximum* of four steps. Players who use one or more of the four key positions to solve problems with existing strokes can reduce the process to two steps or even one step.

After the sequences, the chapter presents a series of key images for learning to execute your volleys in match play. Once you have worked through the teaching progressions and the key images, you should go to the chapters on progressive stroke development and court movement. These two chapters will show you a series of progressive drills, exercises, offcourt visualizations, and intermediate competitive games that will allow you to develop the full potential of your volleys and show you how to hit them consistently under pressure in match play.

FOREHAND VOLLEY STROKE SEQUENCE

VISUAL TENNIS FOREHAND VOLLEY MODEL

Study the forehand stroke sequence above. The sequence demonstrates the core elements in all classic forehand volleys. Note there is no independent hitting-arm motion. The shoulder turn prepares the racket. The palm of the hand and the rotation of the torso then push the racket foreword through the contact.

Unlike the ground strokes, where the most effective key tends to be the finish position, the effective key for the volley is usually some version of the image of the contact point. Because of the limited stroke pattern, if the contact point is correct, the finish will take care of itself on the volley instead of the other way around. Early contact is the key to handling the pace of the oncoming shot, reflecting that pace into your volley, and making precise ball placements. It is what gives a volley that effortless quality characteristic of the great attacking players.

Forehand Volley Key Positions and Images

The following section presents the four key positions for mastering the Visual Tennis forehand volley. Use the checkpoints to create the physical model for each position and a corresponding kinesthetic image of how each position looks and feels inside your mind's eye. This should be done without the ball. Work until you can execute the swing pattern naturally and automatically without the ball, passing accurately through each of the key positions. Take the time at the start of your work to become comfortable with the checkpoints and you will find that you will develop the stroke rapidly and effortlessly on the court.

Following the key positions are three of the most effective key images for the forehand volley. As with the ground strokes, the keys provide a systematic method for creating and sustaining mental focus under the pressure of match play. Particularly at the net, where everything happens twice as fast, anxiety and fear can dominate your mental processes, making concentration impossible. Because you can visualize key images even at the high speed of net play, the key system allows you to stay focused and achieve consistent execution on your volleys. Test and develop your keys according to the chapter on progressive stroke development.

FOREHAND VOLLEY KEY POSITIONS

Key Position 1: Ready Position

1. **Shoulders:** Your shoulders are parallel to the net. Your upper body is straight up and down from the waist. You bend at the knees, and not at the waist.

2. **Hitting arm:** Your hitting arm is positioned so that your elbow tucks in toward your waist. Your hands are slightly above waist level. Wait with the forehand grip.

3. **Racket:** The tip of the racket is even with the top of your head. This high racket position is a key difference between the ready position on the ground strokes and the ready position on the volley.

4. **Legs:** Your legs are slightly wider than shoulder width. Your knees are flexed, and your weight is slightly forward on the balls of your feet.

Close your eyes and visualize details of being in the correct ready position. Notice how the position feels. Make the image and the feeling correspond in your mind.

Work with the key image of the ready position if

1. you feel off balance at the net, or

2. you feel slow starting your volley motion or getting your racket to the turn position.

Key Position 2: Turn Position

1. **Shoulders:** Your shoulders have rotated at least 45 degrees, half or slightly more than on the ground strokes. Note that your shoulders, arm, and racket have moved as a unit.

2. **Hitting arm:** Your hitting arm is set in the double-bend position, with the elbow in and the wrist slightly back. It has rotated in position with the shoulder turn. You position the racket with no independent backswing with the arm.

3. **Racket:** The edge of the racket is even with the *front* edge of your shoulders. The shaft of the racket is 45 degrees to the court surface. The top of the racket is even with the top of the your head. The face of the racket is vertical to the court.

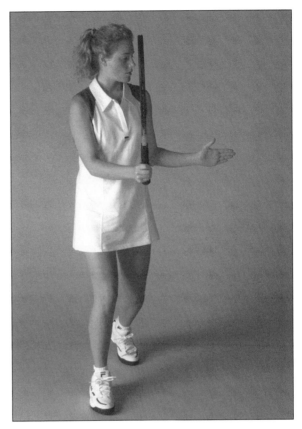

4. **Legs:** Both feet have steped or pivoted sideways. Your weight is on your right, or pivot, foot. You use the toes of your left foot for balance. Your knees are still flexed.

Start in the ready position and move to the turn. Establish the position physically using the checkpoints and then create the mental image.

Work with the key image of the turn if

1. you feel you are overswinging or muscling the ball,
2. you find that you hit the ball with your arm and wrist, or
3. you feel rushed and unprepared for the hit and the ball seems to get on top of you.

FOREHAND VOLLEY KEY POSITIONS

Key Position 3: Contact Point

1. **Shoulders:** Your shoulders have rotated back toward the net, pushing the arm and racket to the contact and generating power automatically through the course of the motion.

2. **Hitting arm:** Your palm and your back, or right, shoulder have pushed the racket head forward to the contact point. Your arm remains in the double-bend position with the elbow in and the wrist back. There is no internal arm motion.

3. **Racket:** The racket is now about a foot to a foot and a half in front of your body. The shaft is still at a 45-degree angle to the court, and the racket face is still vertical.

4. **Legs:** You have stepped forward to the ball with your left foot, with your toes parallel along the edge of a line parallel to the target line of the shot. Your weight is forward on the left, or front, foot. Your knees have uncoiled slightly into the ball.

Start in the ready position and move through the turn to the contact point. Establish the position physically using the checkpoints and then create the mental image.

Work with the key image of the contact point if

1. you take the ball late near or behind the edge of the body,
2. the contact feels jarring and the ball seems to overpower you, or
3. your volleys lack pace and you have difficulty hitting winners, even when you volley into the open court.

Key Position 4: Finish Position

1. **Shoulders:** Your shoulders have continued to rotate slightly farther, until they are approaching parallel with the net. Your upper body is still straight up and down from the waist.

2. **Hitting arm:** Your palm and the torso rotation have pushed the hitting arm and racket through the contact point, on the line of the shot. Your wrist has not released, and your arm is still in the double-bend hitting position.

3. **Racket:** The racket has moved through the ball, with the shaft still at 45 degrees and the face of the racket vertical to the court. The butt of the racket has moved forward slightly past the edge of your left, or opposite, hip.

4. **Legs:** Your weight is now fully forward on your left, or front, foot, and you have come up on the toes of your right foot for balance. Your knees are still slightly flexed.

Start in the ready position and move through the turn and the contact point to the finish. Establish the position physically using the checkpoints and then create the mental image.

Work with the key image of the finish if

1. your motion feels more like a ground stroke,
2. you tend to finish with the racket high and with too long a follow-through, or
3. you consistently overhit.

KEY IMAGE 1: CONTACT POINT FROM THE PLAYER'S PERSPECTIVE

Because the contact point is the central aspect of a good technical volley, keying on this image is usually the most effective way to produce the shot in match play. We show this image from the perspective of how you will probably see yourself in your mind's eye, from slightly over your shoulder and behind. Note that the shaft of the racket is at about 45 degrees to the court. The face of the racket is perpendicular. Your arm is tucked in toward your waist at the elbow, with the wrist laid back in the double-bend hitting position. Your right shoulder is rotating forward so that it is solidly behind the shot. Finally, the contact itself is roughly a foot ahead of your body. You may want to visualize the entire key or focus on one aspect, such as the position of the racket or the hitting position of the arm.

KEY IMAGE 2: CROSS STEP TO THE BALL

Once you have mastered the fundamental elements of the forehand volley, it is possible to produce the entire stroke simply by keying the cross step to the ball. This is often the most effective key for the high speed of match play. Using this key, your shoulders, racket, and feet move as a unit to the contact point.

In the ready position, imagine that the butt of the racket and the tip of your left foot are attached to each other by a steel rod. You can see that with the racket and foot attached, your shoulders will start to turn and the racket will start to move forward automatically as you begin your step. At the contact point, your right shoulder will rotate forward, pushing the racket to early contact as shown in the third frame. Practice the cross step to the contact. As you do, create an image of the motion, of the steel rod connecting your left foot and the butt of the racket, and how it feels to execute the key.

KEY IMAGE 3: USING SHOULDER ROTATION

A common error on the volley is taking the arm and racket back independently, without rotating the body. This makes early contact impossible and reduces the velocity of the shot.

Notice that the hitting arm and racket are already in the double-bend position in the first photo of the ready position. This position is maintained in the second photo. The shoulders have rotated about 45 degrees to the net, positioning the racket at the front edge of the body. The shoulders, arm, and racket turn as a unit. Simply by turning your shoulders you will position the racket correctly. In the third photo, the shoulders have rotated back, with the palm of the hand pushing the arm and racket to the contact point. You can key the entire stroke on the rotation of the shoulders. Establish each of the three positions physically and create a mental image. The key can be any of the three images or a mini-movie of the entire shoulder motion. As you develop the keys, visualize how the motion looks and feels. If you are not using your shoulders to make the turn, work with this key.

UNDERSPIN FOREHAND VOLLEY SEQUENCE

VISUAL TENNIS UNDERSPIN FOREHAND VOLLEY MODEL

The underspin volley is necessary for hitting low volleys and taking the pace off the ball to make a sharply angled placement or a touch volley. It will also add control on routine volleys at shoulder or waist height. The second major advantage of this shot is that it eliminates the need for grip changes at the net because you use the same grip for the backhand volley.

The primary difference in hitting the forehand volley with underspin is the change from the forehand to the continental grip. The grip should be between the eastern forehand and the eastern backhand grip. This means that part of the heel pad of the racket hand is on the top bevel of the frame. The altered grip is the only change required to add underspin to the shot. If you are unsure of the continental grip or are learning it for the first time, refer to the demonstration in chapter 3, "Visual Tennis Grips."

By changing to the continental grip, the face of the racket will automatically be slightly open to the surface of the court at the beginning of the motion. This bevel in the racket-face angle is clearly visible at both the start and completion of the turn. Once you set the angle of the racket face, it remains unchanged throughout the stroke. Thus, the face of the racket remains open at the step to the ball, at the contact point, all the

way through to the finish position. By moving through the ball at this angle, the strings will automatically slide underneath the ball, creating underspin. Imagine the ball as an orange and the racket face as a knife. The knife should slice off the diagonal back third of the ball at contact, as it did with the underspin backhand ground stroke.

Because the biomechanics of the underspin volley are similar to the flat volley, we will not repeat the progression through the key positions and checkpoints. If you have developed a solid basic volley, you can add underspin simply by changing the grip and the angle of the racket through the swing. Make sure that you allow the face to open at the start of the turn. Now complete the motion in the same fashion. Step to the ball, keep the arm in the correct double-bend position, and make early contact.

As you practice moving through the sequence above, create an image or a mini-movie of the open racket face moving through the contact on a straight line. Hitting through the ball is crucial to creating body leverage and pace, and reaching the earliest possible contact point. With the racket face open, however, some players will have the tendency to hit down on the ball, believing this is necessary to create spin. The underspin is, in fact, created by the open face moving through the ball. Hitting down will result in late contact and loss of pace and ball control. Focus particularly on the frames just before and just after contact (fourth and sixth frames). Visualize how this key looks and how it feels. Now test the stroke in controlled drill.

ONE-HANDED BACKHAND VOLLEY SEQUENCE

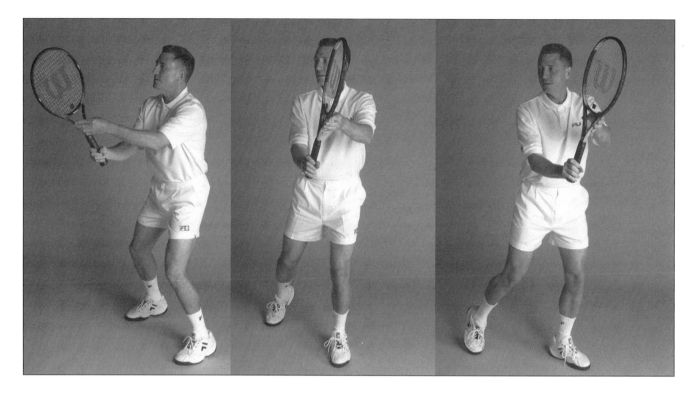

VISUAL TENNIS ONE-HANDED BACKHAND VOLLEY MODEL

The stroke sequence above demonstrates the core elements in the classical one-handed backhand volley. As with the forehand, the shoulder turn positions the racket. The hitting arm and racket move forward through the stroke as a unit, with the torso remaining almost completely sideways. Note that the contact point is in front of the player's body (see the fifth frame). Early contact allows you to use the pace of the oncoming ball to create power and develop precise ball control.

One-Handed Backhand Volley Key Positions and Images

The following sections present the four key positions for mastering the one-handed backhand volley, followed by three key images. First, use the four key positions and the numbered checkpoints that accompany each position to create the physical model of

the stroke. This should be done without the ball. Work until you can execute the swing pattern naturally and automatically without the ball, passing through each of the key positions.

Second, develop your own stroke keys based on the key images and your results on the court. Experiment using different images to help correct your technique when your stroke breaks down. The process for creating your own stroke keys is identical to that for mastering the key positions. First, establish the position physically, referring to the checkpoints that accompany each image. Next, close your eyes and create an image of the position in your mind's eye, giving it as much detail as you can. Notice how the position feels physically and make the image and the feeling correspond in your mind. The three key images for the one-handed backhand volley are the contact point, the cross step to the ball, and the use of the shoulders in the preparation. Try using different stroke keys to find out which works best for you.

ONE-HANDED BACKHAND VOLLEY KEY POSITIONS

Key Position 1: Ready Position

1.   **Racket:** The tip of the racket is about even with the top of your head. As with the forehand volley, this higher racket position is a key difference from the ready position on the ground strokes.

2.   **Shoulders:** Your shoulders are parallel with the net. Your upper body is straight up and down from your waist. The bend is in your knees, not your waist.

3.   **Hitting arm:** Your hitting arm is positioned so your elbow tucks in slightly toward your waist. Your hands are slightly above waist level. Your right forearm is parallel to the court surface. Wait with the forehand grip.

4.   **Legs:** Your legs are slightly wider than shoulder width. Your knees are flexed, and your weight is slightly forward on the balls of your feet.

Close your eyes and visualize yourself with detail in the correct ready position. Notice how the position feels and make the image and feeling correspond in your mind.

Work with the key image of the ready position if

1. you feel off balance at the net, or
2. you feel slow starting your volley motion or getting your racket to the turn position.

Key Position 2: Turn Position

1. **Racket:** The edge of the racket is about even with the front edge of your shoulders. The top of the racket is still even with the top of your head. The shaft of the racket is at about a 45-degree angle to the court surface. The face of the racket is vertical to the court.

2. **Shoulders:** Your shoulders have rotated sideways almost 90 degrees, so they are approaching perpendicular to the net. Your shoulders, hitting arm, and racket have rotated as a unit.

3. **Hitting arm:** You have changed to the backhand grip. Your hitting arm has not moved independently but has swung into position with the shoulder turn. This is the open U position. Your forearm is horizontal to the court, and your wrist is locked. Your upper arm and the racket are at about a 45-degree angle to the court.

4. **Legs:** Your feet have stepped or pivoted sideways. Your weight is on the left, or pivot, foot, and you use the toes of your right foot for balance. Your knees are still flexed.

Move from the ready position to the turn. Establish the position physically using the checkpoints and then create the mental image.

Work with the key image of the turn if

1. you feel you are overswinging or muscling the ball,

2. you find that you hit the ball with your arm and wrist, or

3. you feel rushed and unprepared for the hit and the ball seems to get on top of you.

ONE-HANDED BACKHAND VOLLEY KEY POSITIONS

Key Position 3: Contact Point

1. **Racket:** The racket has moved forward to the ball, meeting it at least a foot in front of the edge of your right shoulder. The angle of the racket to the court has not changed. The shaft is at about a 45-degree angle to the court, and the face is still vertical.

2. **Shoulders:** Your shoulders have rotated only slightly. They have stayed basically sideways, keeping your weight behind the ball while your arm and racket have moved forward.

3. **Hitting arm:** Your hitting arm has moved forward to the ball as a unit, still in the open U position. Your forearm is still horizontal to the court, and your wrist is still locked.

4. **Legs:** Your right foot has stepped forward to the ball so that your toes are parallel along the edge of a line which is parallel to the target line of the shot. Your weight is forward on the right foot. Your knees have uncoiled slightly into the ball.

Move from the ready position through the turn to the contact point. Establish the position physically using the checkpoints and then create the mental image.

Work with the key image of the contact point if

1. you take the ball late near or behind the edge of the body or you feel that you hit with movement in your wrist, or

2. the contact feels jarring and the ball seems to overpower you, or

3. your volleys lack pace and you have difficulty hitting winners, even when you volley into the open court.

Key Position 4: Finish Position

1.   **Racket:** The racket has continued straight out through the line of the shot, about a foot and a half past the contact point. The shaft is still at a 45-degree angle to the court, and the face is still vertical. The butt of the racket has traveled foreward just past the edge of your right hip.

2.   **Shoulders:** You finish the stroke with a minimum of shoulder rotation. Your front, or right, shoulder has rotated back slightly past perpendicular with the net, at most. Your upper body is still straight up and down from the waist.

3.   **Hitting arm:** Your hitting arm has moved forward to the ball in the same open U position, with no internal movement through the course of the stroke. The racket and your upper arm are both 45 degrees to the court. Your forearm is still horizontal to the court, and you have not released your wrist.

4.   **Legs:** Your weight is now fully forward on your right, or front, foot. You have come up on the toes of your rear foot for balance. Your knees are still slightly flexed.

Move from the ready position through the turn and the contact to the finish position. Establish the position physically using the checkpoints and then create the mental image.

Work with the key image of the finish if

1. your motion feels more like a ground stroke,
2. you tend to finish with the racket high and with too long a follow-through, or
3. you consistently overhit.

KEY IMAGE 1: CONTACT POINT FROM THE PLAYER'S PERSPECTIVE

As with the forehand volley, the most effective key for the backhand volley is usually the image of the contact point. If the contact is early, the shot will have body leverage and natural pace. You will control the placement of the ball, and the stroke will feel effortless. This image is shown from the perspective you will probably see yourself in your mind's eye.

Note that the shaft of the racket makes an angle of about 45 degrees to the court, as does the upper arm. The face of the racket is perpendicular. Your forearm is horizontal and your wrist is locked. Finally, you make contact with the ball at least a foot in front of your right shoulder. Establish the position physically and create the mental image.

KEY IMAGE 2: CROSS STEP TO THE BALL

Once you have mastered the core elements of the one-handed back-hand volley, you can key the stroke on the cross step to the ball. This is usually an effective key at the high speed of match play, but it requires that you build up a solid basic pattern in controlled drill. Then when you make the cross step the other elements of the motion remain correct. This key allows you to execute the backhand volley with one quick step in match play.

Visualize that the butt of the racket and the tip of your right, or front, foot are connected by a steel rod and therefore must move forward together to the ball. As you begin the step, you will automatically turn and position the racket at the edge of your front shoulder. As you complete the step, the arm and racket move forward as a unit from your shoulder. This results in contact in front of the plane of the body, with your weight moving into the shot. Practice the cross step in controlled drill and, as you do, visualize the image of the butt of the racket and the foot moving forward and how it feels to execute the motion.

KEY IMAGE 3: USING SHOULDER ROTATION

A common error on the backhand volley is executing the backswing with the arm and the racket, taking them back without turning. As this sequence shows, the arm and racket stay in virtually the same position throughout the motion. The preparation and the forward motion both stem from a unitary body rotation. In the ready position, your elbow is in toward your waist, and your forearm is horizontal, or parallel, to the court surface.

To make the turn, rotate your shoulders sideways. Your arm and racket will then move as a unit. Your elbow is still bent and points in, and your forearm remains horizontal. The upper arm and racket are at about a 45-degree angle to the court, resembling the open U position. Maintain this relationship at the contact point. Your hitting arm and racket have swung forward like a gate on the hinge of your shoulder, with your elbow bent and your forearm still parallel to the court. The hitting arm and the racket do not move independently. Create a mental image or mini-movie of how it looks and feels to execute the key.

UNDERSPIN BACKHAND VOLLEY SEQUENCE

VISUAL TENNIS UNDERSPIN BACKHAND VOLLEY MODEL

The basic biomechanics of the underspin volley are identical to the flat volley demonstrated earlier with the exceptions of the change of grip and racket-face angle. We need not repeat here the progression through the key positions and the checkpoints. If you have developed a solid flat volley, you can add underspin by simply altering the angle of the racket face at the start of the turn. The other key elements are the same. You generate the turn from your shoulders and use no backswing. Your hitting arm and racket stay in the same position throughout the stroke, and you make contact well in front of your right shoulder.

For the underspin backhand volley use the same continental grip you used for the underspin forehand volley. Most players find it easier to produce underspin with this grip than with the more extreme eastern backhand because it is easier to hit through the line of the shot. By hitting both volleys with the same grip, you eliminate the grip shift at the net, a major advantage in playing attacking tennis.

To create underspin, you must set the angle of the racket face correctly at the start of the turn. You can see in the second frame that the racket face is already slightly open. You accomplish this by rotating the wrist and forearm slightly backward as the motion starts. By the time you complete the turn, the face of the racket is beveled at a 30- to 45-degree angle to the court. Once you set the angle of the racket face, it remains unchanged through the remaining course of the

motion. Thus the racket face remains slightly open at the step to ball, at the contact point, and at the finish position. It moves straight through the motion on the line of the shot, rather than downward. The angle of the racket face slides under the ball, creating underspin automatically, just as it does on a slice backhand ground stroke.

You can use the underspin backhand volley to make any shot you previously made with the flat volley. The underspin gives you more control of speed and placement. Underspin is also a necessity for low volleys, sharply angled volleys, or touch volleys. Therefore, you hit all backhand volleys with the same basic biomechanics.

Because it shares the basic technical characteristics of the flat volley, most of the same keys apply equally well to the underspin variation. These include the image of the early contact point, the image of the shoulder turn, and the cross step to the ball.

As with the underspin forehand volley, one additional key is important to solid execution. This is the image of hitting through the ball on a line. Because the racket face is open at the turn on the underspin volley, some players will tend to hit *down* rather than *through*. The result is late contact, a loss of body leverage, and, therefore, poor ball control and reduced pace. It is the angle of the racket face that creates the spin, not the downward angle of the swing plane. As you practice moving through the sequence above, create a mental image or a mini-movie of the open racket face moving through the contact on a straight line. Focus particularly on the frames just before and just after the contact, and visualize how this image looks and feels.

TWO-HANDED BACKHAND VOLLEY STROKE SEQUENCE

VISUAL TENNIS TWO-HANDED BACKHAND VOLLEY MODEL

The stroke sequence above demonstrates the core elements in the classical two-handed backhand volley: compact preparation using only the shoulder turn, and the use of the back, left arm, and shoulder to generate the stroke.

Two-Handed Backhand Volley Key Positions and Images

The following sections present the four key positions for mastering the two-handed backhand volley, followed by three key images. First, use the four key positions and the numbered checkpoints that accompany each position to create the physical model of the stroke. Work until you can execute the swing pattern naturally and automatically without the ball, passing through each of the key positions.

Second, develop your own stroke key system. The most effective key for most players for the two-handed backhand volley is the early contact key, which creates effortless power and good ball control. The second key is cross step to the ball, which allows you to produce the entire stroke pattern by keying on a single step to the ball. With this key, your racket, shoulders, and legs move as a unit, enabling you to execute solid technical volleys in the rapid-fire exchange of net play. The third key is shoulder rotation. A fatal error at the net is taking the arm and racket back independently rather than allowing the shoulder turn to swing them into position. Working with this key helps you establish the role of body rotation in the stroke. Try using different stroke keys to find out which works best for you depending on your technique weaknesses.

TWO-HANDED BACKHAND VOLLEY KEY POSITIONS

Key Position 1: Ready Position

1. **Racket:** The tip of the racket is about even with the top of your head. Your hands are together in the two-handed backhand grip. Wait with this grip for both the forehand and backhand volley.

2. **Shoulders:** Your shoulders are parallel with the net. Your upper body is straight up and down from your waist. You bend at your knees, not your waist.

3. **Hitting arm:** Your left arm is positioned so that your elbow tucks in toward your waist, with your wrist laid back. Both your forearms are parallel to the court.

4. **Legs:** Your legs are slightly wider than shoulder width. Your knees are flexed, and your weight is forward on the balls of your feet.

Close your eyes and visualize yourself in the correct ready position. Notice how the position feels and make the image and feeling correspond in your mind.

Work with the key image of the ready position if

1. you feel off balance at the net, or
2. you feel slow starting your volley motion or getting your racket to the turn position.

Key Position 2: Turn Position

1. **Racket:** The edge of the racket is even with the front edge of your shoulders. The shaft of the racket is at a 45-degree angle to the court, and the face of the racket is vertical.

2. **Shoulders:** Your shoulders have turned almost 90 degrees until they approach perpendicular to the net. Your shoulders, hitting arm, and racket have rotated as a unit.

3. **Hitting arm:** Your hitting arm has not moved independently but has swung into position automatically with your shoulder turn. Both forearms are horizontal to the court. Your left wrist is slightly laid back. This is the classic double-bend hitting-arm position, which is almost identical to the one you use for the forehand volley.

4. **Legs:** Both feet have stepped or pivoted sideways. Your weight is on the left, or pivot, foot. Use the toes of your right foot for balance. Your knees are still flexed.

Start in the ready position and move to the turn. Establish the position physically using the checkpoints and then create the mental image. Imagine how the position looks and especially how it feels.

Work with the key image of the turn if

1. you feel you are overswinging or muscling the ball,

2. you find that you hit the ball with your arm and wrist, or

3. you feel rushed and unprepared for the hit and the ball seems to get on top of you.

TWO-HANDED BACKHAND VOLLEY KEY POSITIONS

Key Position 3: Contact Point

1.   **Racket:** Your left arm has pushed the racket forward to the ball, with contact at least a foot in front of your body. The shaft is at a 45-degree angle to the court, and the face of the racket is still vertical.

2.   **Shoulders:** Your left hand and left shoulder have generated the hit by rotating forward and around, pushing your left arm and racket forward to the contact point.

3.   **Hitting arm:** Your hitting-arm position is unchanged at the contact, with your elbow in and your wrist still laid back. Your shoulders, arm, and racket have generated the shot by moving forward as a unit. The right arm adds only secondary support.

4.   **Legs:** You have stepped forward with your right foot to the ball, with the toes parallel along a line. This line is parallel to the target line of the shot. Your weight is forward on your front foot. Your knees have uncoiled slightly into the ball.

Start in the ready position and move through the turn to the contact. Establish the position physically using the checkpoints and then create the mental image. Visualize how the position looks and especially how it feels.

Work with the key image of the contact point if

1. you take the ball late near or behind the edge of your body,
2. the contact feels jarring and the ball seems to overpower you, or
3. your volleys lack pace and you have difficulty hitting winners even when you volley into the open court.

Key Position 4: Finish Position

1. **Racket:** The racket has moved through the contact point to the finish. The shaft is still at a 45-degree angle to the court, and the face is still vertical to the court. The butt of the racket has continued foreward just past the edge of your right hip.

2. **Shoulders:** Your shoulders have continued to rotate slightly farther past the contact point until they are almost parallel to the net. Your upper body is still straight up and down at the waist.

3. **Hitting arm:** Your hitting arm has pushed the racket through the contact point to the finish position, along the line of the shot. Your arm and racket have not moved internally, and

your hitting-arm position remains unchanged. Your elbow is still bent, and your wrist is laid back.

4. **Legs:** Your weight is now fully forward on your right, or front, foot. You have come up on the toes of your left, or rear, foot for balance. Your knees are still slightly flexed.

Move from ready position through the turn and the contact to the finish. Establish the position physically using the checkpoints and then create the mental image. Imagine not only how the position looks but how it feels.

Work with the key image of the finish if

1. your motion feels more like a ground stroke,
2. you tend to finish with the racket high and with too long a follow-through, or
3. you consistently overhit.

KEY IMAGE 1: CONTACT POINT FROM THE PLAYER'S PERSPECTIVE

As with all volleys, early contact is the most powerful key for the two-handed backhand. The image here is shown from the player's perspective, from over the shoulder and slightly behind. Note that the shaft of the racket is at about a 45-degree angle to the court. The face of the racket is vertical. The elbow of your left, or hitting, arm is slightly bent, and your wrist is laid back. This is the mirror image of the double-bend hitting-arm position on the forehand volley. Your left shoulder has rotated forward, pushing your arm and the racket to the ball and creating natural body leverage. Finally, you make contact about a foot in front of your body. Establish the contact point physically and create a mental image.

KEY IMAGE 2: CROSS STEP TO THE BALL

As with all volleys, you can key the two-handed backhand volley on the cross step to the ball. This key allows you to execute the shot consistently in high-speed exchanges. With the step, your shoulders, arm, and racket all move as a unit to the ball. Using this key requires mastery of the basic elements. You should use it only when you have firmly established muscle memory for the stroke.

Visualize that the butt of the racket and the tip of your right, or front, foot are attached to each other by a steel rod and therefore must move forward together to the ball. As you begin the step, you will automatically turn and position the racket at the edge of your front shoulder. As you complete the step, the arm and racket move forward as a unit from your shoulder in the correct hitting arm position. This results in contact in front of the plane of the body, with your weight moving into the shot. Practice the cross step in controlled drill and, as you do, visualize the image of the butt of the racket and the foot moving forward and how it feels to execute the motion.

KEY IMAGE 3: USING SHOULDER ROTATION

To hit a two-handed volley correctly, you must use shoulder rotation to prepare and drive the shot while your hitting arm stays in the same position. Your arm and racket never go back independently—you move them in unison with your shoulders.

As the first image shows, your shoulders start parallel to the net. In the second image, your shoulders have turned to the ball so that they are at an angle approaching 90 degrees to the net. By making this rotation, you swing your hitting arm and racket into correct position. In the third image, your shoulders have rotated back toward the parallel position, pushing your hitting arm and racket forward to the ball. The result is early contact and natural power. Move through the motion several times as shown, keying on the role of your shoulders. As you do, create a mental image or a mini-movie of the movement. Imagine how the motion looks and feels in your mind's eye.

OVERHEAD SEQUENCE

VISUAL TENNIS OVERHEAD MODEL

This section demonstrates the Visual Tennis model for the overhead, the final component in developing a solid net game. The lob is an effective shot against net players, particularly in doubles, because it tests the reliability of the net player's overhead. To be an effective net player, you must be able to put away overheads from inside the service line and hit aggressive shots from deeper positions to stay ahead in the point. A defensive player who uses the lob effectively knows that below high levels of play few overheads can stand this test. A player forced to hit difficult overheads can lose confidence and commit a series of unforced errors. No matter how well you volley, smart opponents can neutralize your ability to attack if your overhead is not reliable. Using the Visual Tennis method, you will learn to develop this vital component of effective net play and use your key images to execute it with precision and consistency under pressure.

The above sequence demonstrates the core elements shared by all great overheads. These include an immediate shoulder turn to begin the preparation, a full racket drop, great extension at contact, and a relaxed, full motion.

Compared to the motion for the serve, as demonstrated in the next chapter, the motion of the racket during the backswing on the overhead is much more compact. From the ready position (see first frame), the player simply turns his or her shoulders, taking the racket straight back to initiate the preparation. From here the racket moves upward until the elbow and racket position are high and the racket naturally falls into the drop position (see third frame). Many players make the mistake of dropping the hitting arm and the racket down toward the court at the start of the motion, as if they were hitting a serve from a stationary position. This wastes precious time and makes movement to the ball more difficult. The compact Visual Tennis preparation presented in the key positions will maximize your ability to hit your best overheads from anywhere on the court.

The following sections present the four key positions for mastering the overhead, followed by two additional key images.

OVERHEAD KEY POSITIONS

Key Position 1: Ready Position

1. **Shoulders:** Your shoulders are parallel to the net. Your upper body is straight up and down from the waist. Your bend is in the knees, not at the waist.

2. **Hitting arm:** Your hitting arm is positioned so that the elbow tucks in toward the waist. Your hands are slightly above waist level. Wait with the forehand grip or the continental if you have learned to volley with one grip.

3. **Racket:** The tip of the racket is even with the top of your head. This high racket position is a key difference between the ready position for the overhead and the ready position for the ground strokes.

4. **Legs:** Your legs are slightly wider than shoulder width. Your knees are flexed, and your weight is slightly forward on the balls of your feet.

Close your eyes and visualize yourself with detail in the correct ready position. Notice how the position feels and make the image and the feeling correspond in your mind.

Work with the key image of the ready position if

1. you feel off balance at the net, or
2. you feel slow starting your overhead motion or getting your racket to the turn position, or
3. you feel rushed by the ball.

Key Position 2: Racket Drop

1. **Shoulders:** Your shoulders have rotated about 90 degrees until they are almost perpendicular to the net. Note that your shoulders, arm, and racket have moved as a unit, which completes a significant portion of the racket preparation.

2. **Hitting arm:** Your hitting arm has made a compact additional upward motion until your elbow reaches a 45-degree angle with the court. At this point your arm and racket fall naturally into the drop position.

3. **Racket:** The edge of your racket is even with your right side. The shaft of the racket is perpendicular to the court surface. The face of the racket faces the side fence.

4. **Legs:** Both feet have stepped or pivoted sideways. Your weight is on your right, or pivot, foot, and you are using the toes of your left foot for balance. Your knees are still flexed.

Start in the ready position and move to the turn. Establish the position physically using the checkpoints and then create the mental image.

Work with the key image of the racket drop if

1. you feel your motion has no natural power,
2. you feel you are overswinging or muscling the ball, or
3. you feel rushed and unprepared for the hit and the ball seems to drop on top of you.

OVERHEAD KEY POSITIONS

Key Position 3: Contact Point

1. **Shoulders:** Your shoulders have rotated back toward the net so that they are at about a 45-degree angle. This supplies natural leverage and power. Your upper body is straight up and down from the waist.

2. **Hitting arm:** Your forearm has extended upward from the elbow. At the same time, your palm and forearm have rotated from left to right, turning the racket face forward to the contact point. At contact, you fully extend your arm from the shoulder.

3. **Racket:** The racket is directly above your right shoulder and about a foot to a foot and a half in front of the plane of the your body. The face of your racket is square to the ball or, if you are using the continental grip, at a slight angle.

4. **Legs:** Your left foot has stepped forward to the ball, with the toes parallel along the edge of a line parallel to the target line of the shot. Your weight is forward on the left, or front, foot. Your knees have uncoiled slightly into the ball.

Start in the ready position and move through the turn to the contact point. Establish the position physically using the checkpoints and then create the mental image.

Work with the key image of the contact point if

1. you take the ball below full extension,

2. the contact feels jarring and the ball seems to overpower you, or

3. your overheads lack pace and you have difficulty hitting winners even when you hit into the open court.

Key Position 4: Finish Position

1. **Shoulders:** Your shoulders have continued to rotate farther until they are again parallel with the net. Your upper body is still straight up and down from the waist, and your elbow is still in the double-bend hitting position.

2. **Hitting arm:** Your palm and your torso rotation have pushed your hitting arm and racket through the contact point, on the line of the shot. Your wrist has not released. The palm of your hand is even with the middle of your front leg.

3. **Racket:** The racket has moved through the the line of the shot and then down and across the body. The racket hand finishes in the middle of the front leg.

4. **Legs:** Your weight is now fully forward on your left, or front, foot. You have come up on the toes of your right foot for balance. Your knees are still slightly flexed.

Start in the ready position and move through the turn and the contact point to the finish. Establish the position physically using the checkpoints and then create the mental image.

Work with the key image of the finish if
1. your motion feels constricted or tense,
2. your motion lacks power, or
3. you consistently overhit.

KEY IMAGE 1: CONTACT POINT FROM THE PLAYER'S PERSPECTIVE

High contact in front of the body ensures maximum net clearance, power, and accuracy. It provides the difference between a clean winner and an overhead that your opponent can return. To move from the drop to the contact, rotate your palm and forearm from left to right and extend your arm from the high elbow position at the drop. Note several key points. Your arm is straight and directly above your shoulder. The face of the racket is in front of the plane of your body so you make contact slightly out over the court. Establish the position physically and visualize how the key looks and feels inside your mind's eye.

KEY IMAGE 2: FINISH POSITION FROM THE PLAYER'S PERSPECTIVE

The follow-through on the overhead is crucial to maximizing racket-head acceleration. A common tendency is to overhit the overhead by tightening up the arm muscles. This leads to a short, constricted follow-through and a loss of shot velocity. If you find that your follow-through is consistently short, this should be a primary key for you. At the end of the motion, your racket hand should touch down on your left, or front, leg, as shown. This full finish will keep your arm relaxed and maintain a flowing swing. Establish the position physically and visualize the image and the feeling of the key.

CHAPTER 7

THE SERVE

There is a saying in tennis that you are only as good as your serve. If you always hold your serve in match play, the worst that can happen is that every set will go to a tiebreaker. And if you always hold your serve, with just one service break, you will win every set. All great players are able to win most of their service games. The ability to hold serve at higher levels of competition is usually what determines how far a player can progress competitively in the game.

Unfortunately, at the recreational level, the opposite is often true—many players are only as bad as their serves. Unable to hold serve consistently, they are under continuous pressure to break serve just to stay even in the match. Often they hit the first serve as hard and flat as they can. But because it rarely goes in, they hit a tentative, pushed second serve. This destroys the advantage of serving. It allows the opponent to take the offensive from the first ball. It turns what should be the most positive aspect of the game into a consistent liability.

A certain confidence and sense of rhythm come from playing good service games. Knowing you can hold serve, allows you to focus on the returns and shot combinations that can break your opponent. After a break you can play the remainder of the set almost on automatic pilot. Most recreational players, and many competitive players as well, never achieve this frame of mind.

CORE ELEMENTS

As with other strokes, good technical execution of the core elements of the motion are a prerequisite for effective and consistent serving. But the serve differs in a fundamental way from every other shot in tennis. When you serve, you are not hitting an incoming ball. Because the server starts the point with the ball in his or her hand, nothing happens until the server makes it happen. An incoming serve may have an initial velocity of more than 100 miles per hour. A service toss is traveling less than 10 miles per hour.

Most players fail to realize what this absence of significant incoming ball velocity means for the biomechanics of the motion. In a ground stroke or a volley, the velocity of the ball produces significant impact at contact. Even though you should feel smooth hitting these strokes, a minimum level of muscle tension is required to withstand the impact of the ball. Much of the velocity of your shot is already inherent in the incoming ball.

On the serve a similar collision does not occur between the racket and the ball. Instead, you must generate initial velocity through the service motion, which requires greater racket-head acceleration than the motion you use for ground strokes or volleys. The key to maximizing the racket-head acceleration on the serve is a relaxed, full motion. Most recreational players take the level of muscle tension required for ground strokes and carry it over into the service motion. Or worse, in an attempt to increase the speed of the serve, they tense up and muscle the ball. The result is a stiff, constricted motion, loss of consistency and control, and often a reduction in pace.

If you look at the path of the racket on the serve, you will see that it is longer than the path of the swing on the ground strokes. This long, full motion—with a full racket drop—produces maximum racket-head acceleration at the contact point. This is the primary power source on the serve. Besides the swing path, two other sources produce natural power—the rotation of the shoulders and hips through the motion, and the coiling and uncoiling action of the legs.

Body Rotation

The second power source, body rotation, occurs automatically if the player begins the motion with the shoulders positioned correctly. The basic service motion should begin with the shoulders perpendicular to the net. This shoulder position is similar to the position taken at the completion of the turn on the ground strokes. As with the ground strokes, the correct shoulder rotation will then occur naturally because of the swing pattern. Most recreational players unknowingly eliminate this source of free power by standing with the shoulders open to the net in the ready position.

The ultimate potential of shoulder rotation as a power source in the service motion can be seen in delivery of players such as Pete Sampras and John McEnroe. In the mid-1980s, McEnroe took body rotation to a new level. What set his serve apart was his starting stance, with both feet along the edge of the baseline and the toes of his rear foot turned away from, or slightly open to, the baseline. With this stance, McEnroe's body naturally turned during his windup until his back was almost parallel to the net. As the racket came forward to the ball and his shoulders and hips rotated from this position, he came close to doubling the body rotation in his delivery.

Although Pete Sampras is widely acknowledged to have one of the greatest serves in tennis history, what has gone largely unrecognized is the similar role of body rotation in his motion. High-speed video analysis shows that the alignment of his feet in his starting stance is only slightly less extreme than McEnroe's. Although his shoulders start perpendicular to the net, Sampras places his back foot well behind him, with his toes open, or turned away from the baseline. As he begins his windup, the alignment of his stance causes his torso to rotate automatically so that his shoulders are parallel to a line drawn across his toes and his back turned until it almost faces the net. As he uncoils from this position, Sampras vastly increases the shoulder and hip rotation in his serve. This increase in body leverage helps account for the seemingly effortless power in his delivery, as well as his remarkably high serving percentage.

In the section on the advanced serve, Visual Tennis presents a model for the starting stance based on Sampras's motion. After mastering the basic motion, you can learn how to develop similar increased rotation automatically.

Use of the Legs

After the shoulders, the third and final power source in the service motion is the legs. The correct role of the legs in the serve is debated. One view is that you maximize power on the serve by stepping through the shot with the back, or right, leg. By doing so, however, you destroy the timing of your body rotation. Your hips and shoulders fall out of sync with the racket. They rotate too early and get ahead of the rest of the motion, so that by the time the racket gets to the ball, you have wasted a significant body leverage.

As Pete Sampras shows here, modern pros generate power by coiling their legs early in the service motion.

The idea behind the step theory is to get the body into the shot. Unfortunately, it produces the opposite result. Virtually no pro player follows this pattern. Instead they rely on the coiling of the legs and knees. The principle is the same as for the ground strokes—coil the quadriceps by maximizing the knee bend. These powerful muscles will release into the ball as a natural consequence of the swing.

By using your knees in this way, you will automatically spring upward into the ball. When you properly coil your knees instead of cross stepping with your back foot, you will land on your *front* foot and your back leg will kick away from your body for balance. This footwork pattern, sometimes called the *thrust* or the *hop*, is the dominant technique on the pro tour. Players who use it include most of the great servers in the modern game—Pete Sampras, John McEnroe, Ivan Lendl, Stefan Edberg, Martina Navratilova, and Steffi Graf, among others. Although nowhere in the teaching and coaching literature can we find a systematic presentation of this pattern, great players have all developed similar patterns through observation and unconscious visual learning. In the section on the advanced serve, Visual Tennis presents the key images for developing this footwork pattern.

The Toss

Another confusing issue in serving theory is the height of the ball toss. According to a widely publicized view, the correct toss should be low so that the player can strike the ball at the top of the toss, or even on the way up. The problem is that the average player finds this model almost impossible to follow. Again, despite the popularlity of the theory, almost no top players in the modern game use this toss.

The player usually cited as a model for the low toss is Roscoe Tanner, a top American player in the 1970s and early 1980s. Tanner was widely known for the velocity of his serve, clocked on radar at 140 miles per hour. His low service toss contributed to the speed of his serve. With the low toss, Tanner had little time to hit so he executed the service motion rapidly. This, in turn, led to increased racket-head speed, which produced his notable ball velocity.

To execute the motion as quickly as Tanner did, a player must be extremely loose and relaxed. As noted earlier, every player finds this difficult on the serve. The low toss tends to compound the problem. The average player, eager to get the racket around, tends to tense up, hindering the effect he or she is trying to achieve. Experience shows that few players have the natural athletic ability to execute the service motion quickly. They are simply not capable of completing the full motion in such a brief internal.

According to the low-toss theory, a higher ball toss is much more difficult to time. The argument is that as the ball starts to drop, it begins to accelerate, and this change in speed makes timing the contact difficult. But this claim ignores obvious facts about the average tennis player's ability. The speed of the ball during the toss, perhaps 10 miles per hour, is much slower than the velocity of an incoming ground stroke. A player struggling with timing on the serve because of a low toss often has no trouble timing incoming shots that are traveling 5 or 10 times faster.

A high service toss is actually easier to time. It is the key to a relaxed and rhythmic motion. Again, the swing path on the serve is much longer than on ground strokes. To complete the motion smoothly and with technical precision takes time. A high toss gives the player the chance to do this.

A high toss is also critical because it allows the player to develop the advanced footwork pattern that leads to maximum power and spin. If you doubt this, observe the ball tosses of players on the world tour. The majority of professional players have high tosses and hit the ball somewhere on its way down. Video analysis of Sampras shows that his toss drops almost exactly one foot. Other players known for their great serves, such as Becker, Graf, and Navratilova, all toss the ball even higher than that, as much as two feet or more above the contact point.

If these players need a high toss to execute their service motions, imagine how much more important it must be for the majority of tournament and recreational players! The only real issue is how high the toss should be. The key to answering this question is the personal rhythm of the individual server. Every player has a slightly different rhythm to his or her delivery. The trick is to find the toss that suits it best. Some players can move through the motion in less time, stay relaxed, and keep the delivery smooth. Others move through the backswing at a slower pace.

The slower your natural windup, the higher your toss should be. You can determine the correct pace for your serve only by experimentation and feel. You should start by tossing about a foot above the contact point and evaluating the results. If you feel rushed and tense, give yourself additional time by tossing higher. If you feel you are waiting for the ball and your racket is lagging, then lower the toss a little until you find the right tempo.

Use of the Wrist

A final important issue in understanding the core biomechanics of the serve involves the wrist. Players are often told to snap their wrists to increase power and spin. Unfortunately, this is an inaccurate and counterproductive description of what happens at contact. "Snapping the wrist" implies that the wrist breaks so that the palm and the racket head move downward toward the court. High-speed video of any good service motion, however, shows that the rotation of the palm and forearm continues in an inside-out direction. After contact, the racket head turns sideways so that the surface of the strings faces the side fence of the court. Video analysis shows that the effect, called *pronation,* is universal and often extreme among the best players.

As with the "wrap" finish on ground strokes, players and coaches who observe the severe pronation in good serves often consciously try to create the effect. This can result in a radically abbreviated follow-through and a stiff and artificial appearance that may lead to injury.

The motions of top players never stop in an artificially pronated position. Instead, the racket continues across the body, with the arm loose and relaxed, finishing with the palm facing the front of the torso or opposite leg. The pronation we observe in good serving is a natural consequence of a full, high-quality technical motion. On the serve, this includes a full drop, proper movement of the hand and racket head to the contact, and a smooth, natural follow-through.

DEVELOPING AND USING SPIN

As with ground strokes, spin on the serve increases the arc of the ball flight. This means more net clearance and a ball that drops more sharply into the service box. By hitting with spin, you can hit the ball harder and still have confidence that the serve will be in. On the second serve, this confidence is vital. By increasing the rotation on the ball, you can hit this critical shot with unfailing consistency.

The first key to developing effective spin is the grip. By simply changing to a continental grip and making a small adjustment in the basic motion, you will automatically generate spin. The grip change will alter the angle at which the racket face strikes the ball. If you are uncertain about your serve grips or are trying it for the first time, refer to chapter 3 for a demonstration of how to establish a continental grip.

The second key is understanding how and why to vary the spin on your serve. Typically, the types of spin on the serve are described as either slice or topspin. In reality, the type of spin varies along a continuum. If the racket head is traveling in a roughly horizontal line as it approaches the ball, the serve will have more sidespin. The ball will move slightly from right to left and will have a little less kick, bouncing lower after it hits the court. On the other hand, if the angle of the diagonal is more vertical so that the racket head is moving more sharply upward toward the contact, the ball will travel in a straighter path. It will dip more sharply and will tend to kick or bounce higher on contact with the court. This is the topspin serve.

Most recreational players will find the topspin variation easier to master and more effective. The increased arc makes it a higher percentage stroke. The spin produces more net clearance, and the dipping action brings the ball down into the service box. Furthermore, the higher bounce creates problems for opponents on the return. With this spin, you can kick the ball up to shoulder level or even higher, forcing the returning player to hit a high, weak return. Your opponent's only effective counterplay is to take the ball on the rise, before it can get up and on top of him or her. This return is difficult to time consistently. Your opponent is likely to make errors, generating free points for you as the server.

The difference between the first serve and the second serve then is primarily the degree of spin. You can hit the first ball slightly flatter and with a little more pace. The second ball should have more rotation, giving you confidence in your ability to place the ball in the box, even on big points. If you cannot achieve a first-serve percentage of 65 to 75 percent, you should increase the rotation on your first ball to achieve this consistency.

Some people believe you should develop the ability to hit both a topspin serve and a slice serve. They also advocate changing the toss for the different spins. A slice toss is usually more to the right of the server, and lower, making it easier to hit around the side of the ball. The toss for the topspin serve is normally farther back to the left, slightly over the server's head, so that the player can hit up on the ball more radically for topspin.

Again, if we look at the top players, we see that they do not hit two distinct types of spin, much less use two ball tosses. Making such a fundamental change in the motion from ball to ball is difficult. The serve requires rhythmic coordination of the toss and the motion of the body. It is hard enough to develop one consistent service delivery, let alone two. Moreover, an experienced opponent will quickly learn to read changes in the placement of the toss and will know what serve you are planning to hit almost as soon as you do. Instead of having two different service motions, top players develop variations in the degree of spin. They can hit these off the same toss, with the same motion. The variation in spin comes not from changing the service motion but from altering the spot on which the racket makes contact with the ball and the angle of the diagonal along which the racket head is moving.

By using the same toss for every serve, you make it difficult for an opponent to read your delivery. By following this approach, you will actually develop three service variations, not two. You will be able to hit the first serve either fairly flat or with moderate spin. You can hit the second ball with heavier rotation. To keep your opponent guessing and off balance, you can mix this heavier spin with the other two varieties on the first serve. You may also choose to use the heavy-spin serve if you find that your opponent has trouble with the higher bounce.

Once they have mastered these variations, advanced players should also develop the ability to hit slightly more around the side of the ball, off the same basic toss and delivery. This allows a right-handed player to hit wider serves in the deuce court by swinging the ball more radically from right to left. The opposite, of course, applies to a left-hander serving in the ad court.

This ability to mix deliveries and spin is key to effective serving. Some players will hit much better returns off flat, hard serves. Unless you can generate enough velocity to overpower your opponents, hitting flat deliveries may be counterproductive. This is particularly true when playing serve-and-volley tennis, when hard servers frequently find themselves scraping bullet returns off their shoelaces on the first volley. The ball with heavier spin, on the other hand, travels slightly slower, so it allows the net rusher to close to the net faster. The ball with heavy spin also forces higher, floating returns that are much easier to volley. Because of this, Pete Sampras, in hard-court matches, will serve and volley on the second serve as frequently as he does on the first.

In this chapter, we divide into stages the process of learning to serve with the proper mix of power, control, and spin. The first is the mastery of the elements of the basic swing pattern. This is presented in the basic serve sequence, key positions, and key images. The next step is developing the ability to hit spin while staying within the framework of the basic motion.

Although there are occasional exceptions, if you are a beginner you should learn the basic motion for the serve with the forehand grip. This will produce a flat shot, but you will develop a basic feeling for the motion, for striking the ball solidly, and for controlling the direction of the shot. Initially, you should focus on establishing the correct technical swing path. After you have developed a consistent basic swing, you can change to a true serving grip and begin to develop spin.

The additional ball rotation should give the flight of your serve a noticeable arc and cause it to drop more sharply into the serving box. This allows you to hit the serve with confidence and pace, knowing that the ball rotation will keep it in the court. At this point, you can begin to vary the type and the amount of rotation. Typically, you will produce a ball that moves slightly from right to left and kicks up somewhat after the bounce. Most spin serves fall somewhere between pure slice, a ball that rotates sideways from right to left, and pure topspin, a ball that rotates from top to bottom. The ball spins at the angle of the diagonal at which the racket head is moving at contact.

A final factor influencing the type and amount of ball rotation is the placement of the toss. As described in the tossing key on page 145, you should strive to place the toss directly above your hitting shoulder to achieve maximum extension at contact. Many players, however, find that varying the toss placement by a few inches to the left or right makes it easier to achieve different spins. A toss slightly to the right of the shoulder increases the tendency to hit around the ball, generating slice. Similarly, a toss slightly back and to the left lends itself to hitting up and over the ball, generating topspin.

Most players gravitate to one type of rotation or the other. Players such as Pete Sampras, Ivan Lendl, Stefan Edberg, and Boris Becker serve with more of a topspin, kicking rotation. All three toss the ball more to the left than McEnroe, somewhere between the shoulder and the edge of the head. This tossing position is naturally conducive to hitting up and over the ball. It allows them to hit with more velocity and is suited to their powerful styles. McEnroe's toss, classic for a left-handed slice serve, is slightly further to the side, helping produce the wide delivery in the backhand court that was key to the effectiveness of his serve and volley game. Every player should experiment within these parameters, adjusting the toss and spin slightly to find the combination that is most comfortable and effective. After a period of experimentation, however, you should settle on one tossing variation.

The third step is adding advanced footwork and the leg thrust described above, which is the source of the superior power of the great servers in modern game. This is demonstrated in a second photo sequence. We present the advanced starting stance used by players such as McEnroe and Sampras to increase body rotation. By following the progressions, you can bring your serve up to the level of the other parts of your game and learn to win serve consistently in both recreational and tournament play.

In the following section, the core elements for learning or making technical improvements in the basic serve are presented. The service motion is demonstrated in a full sequence, and then broken down into four key positions and, finally, key images.

The key positions are

1. the ready position,
2. the racket drop,
3. the contact point, and
4. the finish position.

These positions and the corresponding images are the building blocks for creating the physical and mental models of the pattern. If you pass through each of the key positions correctly, your entire swing pattern will be correct.

BASIC SERVE SEQUENCE

VISUAL TENNIS BASIC SERVE MODEL

The stroke sequence above demonstrates the basic elements a player must develop to maximize the potential of his or her serve and lay the groundwork for adding advanced elements described in the later part of this chapter. These include a starting stance that automatically generates shoulder rotation, and a full, smooth swing pattern.

You can use the progressions to develop the serve from the ground up, to correct technical difficulties, or to improve serving effectiveness at any level. If you are working to improve an existing motion, the best approach is to video your serve and compare it to the key technical elements in the models. Start by correcting any problems with the core elements in the basic serve. If your basic motion is solid, progress to the advanced serve to develop pro footwork by using the legs and increasing body rotation. Chapter 9, "Progressive Stroke Development," outlines the steps to develop these patterns, correct muscle memory, and use the key images to execute in competition and develop your mental game.

Basic Serve Key Positions

Following are the four key positions for mastering the building blocks of the Visual Tennis basic serve. The model is shown using the continental grip. If you are learning the serve for the first time, you should start with the forehand grip, and proceed to the continental when the model elements are solid. Use the checkpoints to create the physical model for each position and a corresponding kinesthetic image of how each position looks and feels inside your mind's eye. This should be done without the ball. Work until you can execute the swing pattern naturally and automatically without the ball, passing accurately through each of the key positions. Take the time at the start of your work to become comfortable with the checkpoints and you will find that you will develop the stroke rapidly and effortlessly on the court.

BASIC SERVE KEY POSITIONS

Key Position 1: Ready Position

1. **Shoulders:** Your shoulders start perpendicular to the net in the ready position. Stand straight up and down from the waist. Your knees are slightly flexed.

2. **Hitting arm:** Your hitting arm is straight and hangs down from your shoulder in line with your front leg. You can execute the basic serve with either the forehand grip or the continental grip, as shown here.

3. **Racket:** The tip of the racket points straight at the net. The shaft of the racket is parallel with the court, and the face is perpendicular. Your left, or tossing, arm is straight, and the ball is on the face of the racket.

4. **Legs:** Your feet are sideways, parallel to the baseline, with your heels in line. Your weight is equally distributed on both feet, and your knees are slightly flexed.

Close your eyes and visualize yourself with detail in the correct ready position. Notice how the position feels. Make the image and the feeling correspond in your mind.

Work with the key image of the ready position if

1. you have problems generating shoulder rotation as a power source on the serve,

2. you have problems with the position and movement of your tossing arm on your ball toss, or

3. you rush your motion at the start of the delivery.

Key Position 2: Racket Drop

1. **Shoulders:** At the racket drop, your shoulders remain sideways, or perpendicular. You are still straight up and down from the waist.

2. **Hitting arm:** At the completion of the drop, your arm has relaxed and bent at the elbow so the racket can drop fully. Your elbow position is high, about 30-45 degrees with the court. Your upper hitting arm has not gone back behind the plane of your body, staying in line with your shoulders.

3. **Racket:** The tip of the racket has traced a path that is three-fourths of the circumference of a circle, then fallen naturally into the drop position. The racket has dropped all the way down the back. The edge of the racket is in position to scratch the right edge of your body. The tip of the racket is pointing down at the court.

4. **Legs:** Your weight is still forward on the left, or front, foot. Your knees have started to release naturally because of the motion.

Move from the ready position through the still frames to the racket drop. Establish the position physically using the checkpoints and then create the mental image.

Work with the key image of the racket drop if

1. your serve lacks natural power and you feel that you are muscling the ball with your arm and shoulder,

2. your windup feels tight or constricted, or

3. you have difficulty generating power when you try to hit with spin.

BASIC SERVE KEY POSITIONS

Key Position 3: Contact Point

1. **Shoulders:** Your shoulders have started to rotate with the start of the hitting motion and are about 45 degrees to the net. You transfer the power from the rotation naturally into the ball by using the proper stance and swing. Your upper body is straight up and down from the waist.

2. **Hitting arm:** Your forearm has turned with your palm and also extended from the elbow, moving the racket upward to the ball. At contact, your arm is straight and fully extended upward from your shoulder.

3. **Racket:** The racket head is directly above your right shoulder and slightly in front of your front foot so that the contact is over the court and in front of your body. With the continental grip the shaft of the racket will be at a slight angle to the court, indicating that you have struck the ball at an angle for spin.

4. **Legs:** Your knees have naturally released from their coiled position upward into the ball but are still slightly flexed. Your weight is on your front foot, and you are starting to come up on the toes of your back foot. You have not stepped through the shot and remain on balance.

Start in the ready position and move through the still frames to the contact point. Establish the position physically using the checkpoints and then create the mental image.

Work with the key image of the contact point if

1. you have problems with the trajectory or your serve, either low net clearance and a tendency to hit faults into the net or consistently long,

2. you lose power by making contact too close to or behind the plane of your body, or

3. you rush the motion from the racket drop to hit and tend to muscle the ball.

Key Position 4: Finish Position

1. **Shoulders:** Your shoulders have rotated a full 90 degrees from the ready position until they are parallel with the net. Your upper body has remained straight up and down from the waist.

2. **Hitting arm:** Your hitting arm has remained relaxed, carrying the racket all the way through to the finish in a smooth motion. Your right, or racket, hand should touch down in the middle of your left, or front, leg.

3. **Racket:** The racket has accelerated all the way through the hit. The racket head moves out along the line of the shot and then down and across your body. At the finish the racket is on the left side of your left, or front, leg. Pronation has occurred naturally during the motion as a consequence of racket-head acceleration and the contact.

4. **Legs:** Your weight is now fully forward on your left, or front, foot. You have come up on the toes of your right foot for balance. Your knees have uncoiled into the ball but remain slightly flexed.

Start in the ready position and move all the way through the still frames to the finish position. Establish the position physically using the checkpoints and then create the mental image.

Work with the key image of the finish position if

1. your arm feels tight and constricted when you try to generate power,

2. your motion lacks rhythm or consistency, or

3. your serving percentage tends to go down under pressure or on big points.

Basic Serve Key Images

This section presents six key images for developing and executing the basic serve. The first three keys are images of the key positions—the racket drop, the contact point, and the finish position—shown from the player's perspective. These keys are effective not only in producing consistent execution but also in correcting technical problems with the swing itself, as explained later.

The fourth key is for the tossing motion. Without a good toss, it is simply impossible to hit the serve correctly. Many players find the toss the single most difficult obstacle. By keying the motion with the image of the straight-arm position, any player can develop a reliable toss.

The next key is for timing the motion. Assuming the swing pattern is correct, the biggest problems most players face are developing and maintaining the slower rhythm of the stroke compared with ground strokes and volleys and staying relaxed in the excitement of matches. This key shows you how to key the timing of the motion to a three count that will keep the rhythm smooth.

The last key shows you how to generate spin on the basic serve. This is the key to serving aggressively. Spin gives you confidence that you can get both your first and second serves in the court, even under pressure, without holding back your motion. Spin permits you to hit out on the serve and increase your serving percentage and accuracy.

Establish the key physically, referring to the checkpoints that accompany the image. Next, close your eyes and create an image of the key in your mind's eye, giving it as much detail as you can. Now work to master the keys by referring to chapter 9. As you start your service motion, hold the image of the key in your mind and make the motion overlap the image.

Use the keys presented here as a guide to developing your own personal system of serve keys. Determine which keys work best for you based on the weaknesses in your own stroke.

KEY IMAGE 1: RACKET DROP FROM THE PLAYER'S PERSPECTIVE

The primary power source on the service motion is the acceleration of the racket from the drop position up to the contact. Many players, however, fail to achieve a complete drop, diminishing the role of this fundamental factor. As any teaching pro knows, an incomplete drop is a difficult flaw to correct. Working with this key can eliminate the problem from your game. This key is also effective for players who tend to shorten the motion under the pressure of match play. The key is shown from the player's perspective, the angle from which you will see it in your mind when you construct your mental image.

Note that the edge of the racket falls along the side of your body. The tip of the racket points down at the court, and the elbow position is high. Establish the racket drop physically. Now create the mental image. Test the key in controlled drill.

KEY IMAGE 2: CONTACT POINT FROM THE PLAYER'S PERSPECTIVE

High contact is crucial to the service motion. It ensures maximum net clearance and imparts a trajectory that places the ball consistently within the service box. High contact also maximizes body leverage and contributes to shot velocity. At contact the great servers extend themselves from the tip of the toes to the tip of the racket. This key, presented from the player's perspective, helps you achieve this.

To move from the drop to the contact, rotate your palm and forearm, extending the arm from the high elbow position at the drop. Note several key points. Your arm is straight and directly above your shoulder. The face of the racket is in front of the plane of your body so that the contact is slightly out over the court. Establish the position physically and visualize how the key looks and feels inside your mind's eye.

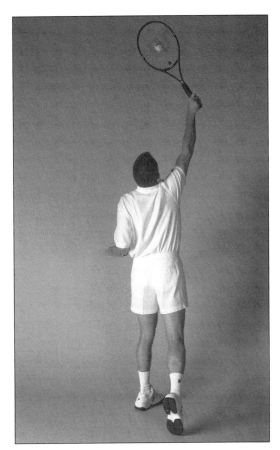

KEY IMAGE 3: FINISH POSITION FROM THE PLAYER'S PERSPECTIVE

As with the ground strokes, the follow-through on the serve is a primary key to maximizing racket-head acceleration throughout the stroke. A common tendency is to overhit the ball by tightening up the arm muscles. This leads to a short, constricted follow-through, which reduces shot velocity rather than increasing it.

If you find that your follow-through is consistently short, make this a primary key. At the end of the motion, your racket hand should touch down on your left, or front, leg as shown. This full finish will allow you to keep your arm relaxed and your swing flowing. Establish the position physically and visualize the image and the feeling of the key.

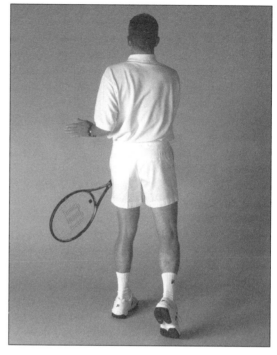

KEY IMAGE 4: THE TOSSING MOTION

Even if you develop a consistent service motion, your delivery will be ineffective without a reliable toss. The key to the toss is keeping it simple. This means keeping your arm straight throughout the motion. Notice that by locking your arm at the elbow and wrist you have no internal movement. Instead, your entire arm simply drops straight down from the hinge of the shoulder and then moves straight up to the ball release and full extension. As your arm begins to drop you should look up to where you are tossing. You should turn your head upward as the tossing motion begins, focusing on the spot where you will deliver the toss. Once the tossing arm is fully extended hold that position until your racket starts forward from the drop.

Instead of throwing or flipping the ball at the release, simply open your hand and allow it to roll off your fingertips. Bending at the elbow or flipping the wrist is what usually causes inconsistency in the toss placement. With your arm straight, execute the tossing motion several times. As you do, create a mental image. As you start the motion, visualize the image of your arm moving straight down and all the way up to full extension.

KEY IMAGE 5: THE THREE COUNT

The best key for keeping the rhythm of the motion even and the arm relaxed is the three count. Start in the ready position. As you start the motion, count to yourself, "One, two, three." The count should be slow and even. "One" should correspond roughly with your arms dropping and the start of the backswing. Count "two" as the backswing continues and the racket drops behind your back. "Three" corresponds with the start of motion upward to the ball, the contact, and the follow-through.

The problem most players face is that somewhere between the two count and the three count they tense up the arm and try to speed up the motion artificially rather than allowing it to accelerate naturally. This constricts the flow of movement and reduces racket-head speed. By keeping the rhythm of the count even, you will keep the rhythm of the serve even as well. This will maximize the speed of your swing.

The height of the toss and the rhythm of the service motion are interrelated. Some players will find that they can move through the motion fairly quickly, stay relaxed, and keep the rhythm even. Others find that if they move quickly, they tense up too much and rush the motion, particularly between the two count and the three count. The slower your individual rhythm, the higher you must toss the ball. You must determine through experimentation the height that works for you and the correspondence between the three count and the parts of your motion. Start by tossing about a foot above your contact point and then evaluate your rhythm. If you feel rushed, increase the height of the toss. If you feel that you are waiting to hit the ball, lower the toss slightly. To create this key, start in the ready position. Now close your eyes and count to yourself. As you count, visualize yourself executing the serve motion in synchronization with the count. Now test the key in controlled drill.

KEY IMAGE 6: DEVELOPING SPIN

Students will often ask their teaching pro to teach them a "spin serve," as if hitting with spin required learning a new and distinct motion. As we have seen, however, hitting with various types and degrees of spin involves only slight variation in the basic service pattern. The biomechanics remain essentially the same. What is different is the angle at which the racket strikes the ball.

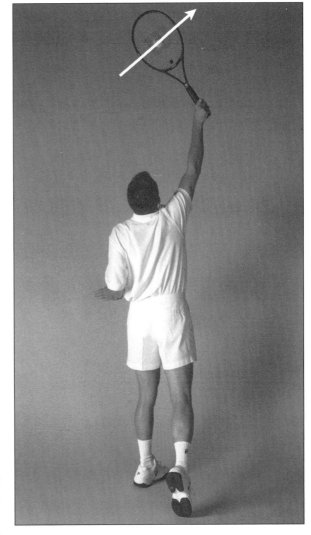

The first step in generating ball rotation is to change to the continental grip. With this grip the racket face will naturally approach the ball at an angle. The only change is that you must rotate your palm and forearm further from left to right as you extend to the contact point. You will make solid contact, and you will naturally generate spin. To create this image, close your eyes and imagine the path of the racket and the point of contact on the ball's surface. Two elements make up the image—the diagonal path of the racket and the spot to the lower left at which the racket contacts the ball. You may see it as a still image of the contact point or a mini-movie of the racket as it moves through the swing. Visualize how the image looks and feels inside your mind's eye.

As you develop your particular serving style, you can experiment with variations on the basic spin. By making the diagonal slightly more vertical, you can generate more topspin. This serve will have more arc and will travel in a straighter line but will also kick up much higher after the bounce. By altering the path of the diagonal line so that it is slightly more horizontal, you can generate more slice. The ball will move more from right to left, bounce lower, and have slightly less pace. Adjust your key images to correspond with the different spins you develop.

Many players who execute their basic service motion with the continental grip produce spin immediately and automatically. But you may find that the ball moves too sharply to the left, with sidespin but little power. To correct this, visualize trying to strike the ball "flatter" with your palm using the continental grip. This will increase the rotation of the forearm from left to right. You will still hit up on the ball at an angle, but this image will produce solid contact and spin, causing the racket head to move on the correct diagonal as it approaches the contact.

ADVANCED SERVE STROKE SEQUENCE

VISUAL TENNIS ADVANCED SERVE MODEL

As noted in the introduction to this chapter, most of the great servers in the modern game use the advanced footwork shown here, known as the thrust or the hop. Every player who wants to develop superior serving ability should progress to the advanced serve but only after achieving solid biomechanics for the basic service motion. This competence should include the ability to hit spin consistently on both the first and second serves.

The distinguishing characteristic of the advanced serve is the increased role of the legs in generating additional power and spin. A key element in the basic service motion is the weight shift forward to the front, or left, foot and the accompanying knee bend. In the advanced serve, you extend this weight shift and increase the knee bend. The uncoiling motion that follows literally propels you upward into the ball. By using your legs more intensively, you create considerable additional leverage, increasing the velocity and ball rotation of your serve.

The key element in the advanced serve is increasing the knee bend at the beginning of the motion, starting when your arms drop. You should continue to increase the knee bend until you complete the backswing. By going down on your knees as far you can, you create the uncoiling action upward into the ball as an automatic consequence of the hitting motion.

As your knees uncoil and your quadriceps release upward into the ball, you simultaneously kick your rear foot back and away from your body. Your rear foot serves as a counterweight, allowing you to launch yourself upward into the ball while remaining on balance and straight up and down at the waist. You then land on your left, or front, foot. This relationship between the feet is crucial for unlocking the added power of the legs and retaining the proper sequence of body rotation into the ball.

If you are continuing to the net, you can take the next step forward with the back foot or simply recover to the ready position for baseline play. In developing this motion it is important that you be able to stop the movement and retain balance after the hop, with your weight still on your front foot. Apart from this enhanced role of the legs, the biomechanics of the motion are unchanged, and the stroke keys from the basic serve apply.

KEY IMAGE I: KICKING BACK WITH THE BACK LEG

As noted in the introduction to this chapter, a common flaw is the tendency to step through the motion with the back leg. This throws off synchronization of the motion, rotates the body too early, and reduces power. This tendency causes much of the serving inconsistency at the recreational and lower competitive levels.

This key will help you control your back foot. It is crucial to the proper use of the legs on the advanced serve. By kicking out and away from the body as the knees uncoil, the back leg serves as a counterweight. It allows you to retain good balance, remain straight up and down from the waist, and achieve full extension at contact. Most important, the leg kick keeps your weight behind the ball. This permits you to take full advantage of the extra body leverage generated by the uncoiling of your legs and still land on your front foot. The sequence of photos of the advanced serve demonstrates this. Watch the good serve-and-volley players and note how they universally land on the front foot before continuing to the net. They can do this only by using the rear leg .

To create this key, start in the ready position. Now drop your arms and bend your knees, going down to whatever is your maximum bend. Then, without continuing the swing or hitting the ball, release your knees so that you hop upward and forward. Land on your front foot. As you do this, kick your rear, or right, leg back and away from your body as shown. Now, repeat this motion, and create a visual image of your right leg as it moves backward. You should be able to land in a balanced position without taking any additional steps.

KEY IMAGE 2: MAXIMIZING BODY ROTATION WITH THE ANGLED STARTING STANCE

A key for getting the most out of your natural ability on the serve is experimenting with your starting stance. As discussed, John McEnroe was the first top player to adjust the angle of his feet in the ready position to increase torso rotation in the motion. Pete Sampras, another of the game's all-time great servers, has developed a variation on this stance with a similar result. The model presented here is based on the Sampras stance, which is slightly less extreme than McEnroe's.

You should experiment with the angled stance only after you have solid basic biomechanics for the motion and have developed advanced use of the legs. If you have mastered these elements, you can use the angled starting stance to augment velocity and spin further still, and do so automatically in the natural course of executing your motion.

The key is simply the proper alignment of your feet and body at the start of the motion. Your front foot should be parallel to the baseline. Set your rear foot about a foot and a half behind you, with your toes open 45 degrees to the baseline. The heel of your front foot is now in line with the arch of your rear foot. Your shoulders remain perpendicular to the net.

As you begin your motion, your torso will naturally turn back away from the net so your hips and shoulders are in line with the stance. No artificial or independent shoulder movement occurs; it happens as a result of the angled alignment. As the racket goes to the ball, your hips and shoulders will naturally increase their rotation through the shot. Nothing in the basic motion or the coiling and uncoiling of your legs changes. These factors work in concert with the added rotation. When you execute the motion properly, you will hear the effect in the sound of the hit. It will simply sound louder and more powerful, almost like a small explosion.

At our tennis school we have exciting results teaching this angled stance to players at many levels—high school and junior players, league players, as well as high-level tournament players. One of the top men's players in northern California who adopted the angled stance put it this way: "It amazed me that one adjustment that seemed so simple could make such a huge impact in my serving effectiveness." Even if your serve is your strength, experimenting with this key can result in significant improvement.

KEY IMAGE 3: MAXIMIZING KNEE BEND

The first step in developing the knee bend key is determining how far you can bend. This will depend on your physical strength and flexibility. Players such as McEnroe, Becker, and Sampras go down until they bend their knees almost at a right angle. Most players cannot match this, but you must find out for yourself. The bend shown is a fairly typical maximum for most players. Try it by letting your arm drop and starting the knee bend. Shift as much weight as you can to the left, or front, foot and see how far down in the knees you can go. Stay on balance without bending over at the waist. Now create the visual image as shown. See yourself from the waist down with your weight on the left, or front, foot with your maximum possible bend. As you start your service motion, hold the image of your knee bend and make your legs overlap the image. Visualize yourself staying down as long as you can. As your swing progresses, you will automatically uncoil upward from your legs. You should land on your front foot on balance, with your rear leg kicking backward.

COURT MOVEMENT

It may be cliche in tennis, but it's true: If you can't get to the ball it doesn't matter how well you can hit it. Court movement is one of the key elements that separates players at one level from those at another. A player may hit the ball with velocity and accuracy but be unable to get into position against better opponents.

The great champions have all been the best or nearly the best movers of their day. Visualize Bjorn Borg tirelessly running down shots, or John McEnroe gliding forward on perfect balance to cut off a volley on what looked like a sure passing shot. With his legs always slightly coiled, Pete Sampras resembles nothing so much as a panther—staying low and moving effortlessly into position to execute one of his beautiful classical stroke patterns. A player like Michael Chang uses speed as a weapon, making up for a lack of overpowering shot making.

Good movement in tennis is not a matter of simple acceleration. Your goal is not to race across a finish line at full speed. The goal is to reach the ball and set up in position to execute a stroke. This means moving rapidly to the ball. But equally important, it means setting up in a balanced hitting position. The goal is to position yourself as if the ball had initially come directly to you.

This chapter shows you the principles of movement to reach this goal—to beat the ball to its destination, arrive on balance, set up properly, and then execute a high-quality classical stroke. This also means learning how—and when—to hit off the back foot, both on the ground strokes and the volleys. As with the Visual Tennis strokes themselves, the key to movement is to reduce the patterns to a few elements and learn to think of them in images that you can use on the court.

MOVING TO GROUND STROKES

Many players are confused about the footwork practiced at the pro level today because so many of the top players hit with a so-called open stance, particularly off the forehand side. Certainly it is true that many, if not most, of the top players do *not* step into the forehand with the front foot, including Pete Sampras on many balls. But commentators mislead us when they use the term *open stance* to describe this pattern. An open stance implies that the body itself is open to the ball with the shoulders facing the net so that the shot is hit primarily with the arm. In reality, the top players who hit off the back foot have excellent turns and achieve hip and shoulder rotation equal to, or even greater than, players who hit with the traditional closed stance.

A clearer explanation of the role of stance and positioning considers the relationship between the feet. As you progress to higher levels and hit the ball harder, you will find it more difficult to arrive at the ball in position to hit. Often you will simply not have time to step into the shot with the front foot. Learning to position with the back foot becomes critical. By learning to position correctly with either foot you can maintain the core biomechanical elements in classical strokes. A classical player should develop the ability to hit off *either* the front foot or the back foot, depending on the situation and personal preference and style.

The following patterns teach you how to prepare, move, and position yourself to the ball with the option to hit off either foot and then recover to the ready position for the next shot. This means learning to reach the ball with the back, or outside, foot. Tournament players often call this "getting behind the ball." The step with the front foot has nothing to do with positioning to hit the ball. When you are behind the ball you have the option of either stepping in or hitting off the back foot.

Complete the Turn

The first component in all Visual Tennis movement patterns is identical to the first component of the stroke itself—the completion of the turn. Late preparation is epidemic in recreational tennis. The efforts of many club players to cover the court are futile because they do not reach the ball in position to hit. This is why the completion of the turn is the critical prerequisite to good movement in the Visual Tennis system.

Some top players separate the body turn from complete racket preparation. But for the rest of us, the failure to establish the racket in the completed turn position at the start of movement is the kiss of death. It would be almost impossible to overemphasize the point. The completion of the turn at the start of the movement pattern increases your chance of executing any shot and is critical to developing consistency, rhythm, and power. Without turning in the proper sequence, you might as well have not made the effort to develop the basic stroke pattern—you will rarely be able to hit it in competitive play.

On the ground strokes, you should strive to complete the turn before the ball crosses to your side or, at the latest, before the bounce. On the volleys, the turn must be more immediate. The process is simple: visualize the key image of the turn, and align your body with the image. If this proves difficult initially, or if you have a habit of delaying the turn, start in the completed turn position *before* your teaching pro or practice partner hits you the ball. When you are moving to the ball and setting up well from the turn position, go back to starting your movement pattern from the ready position.

Keep Steps Short

The second element in good court positioning is the nature of the steps themselves. Initially, you should move with extremely short, fast, choppy steps. Short steps are critical to achieving proper alignment and maintaining balance. Because you often have considerable court to cover, it may seem counterintuitive to take small steps. But the problem with taking large steps is that the increments of movement are too large when you are around the ball. Larger steps will inevitably position you either too close or too far away. You will either be leaning away from the ball or lunging to reach it. You will find it impossible to keep your torso upright, leading to a loss of balance. The natural power, fluidity, and efficiency of the Visual Tennis stroke patterns will be lost.

The split step is critical in attacking the net because it allows a player to recover the ready position, react, and move to the volley.

Small, choppy steps allow you to control precisely the interval of your movement. This is critical to learning to set up behind the line of the flight of the ball. As you learn to move on balance with rapid, small steps you will naturally start to lengthen your stride on longer movement patterns. The key is to stay on balance and to come back to the small, choppy steps around the ball so that you can align precisely.

Align Behind the Ball

Aligning your body accurately with the flight of the ball is the key to consistency and power. As you will see in the following sections, the key image is reaching the ball in the turn position, with the edge of the back foot close to the edge of the line of the ball's flight path. To achieve this, you must practice creating an image of the flight of the oncoming ball. As your opponent hits the ball, visualize its flight as a yellow arc. Extend the internal mental trajectory of the shot to your side of the court. See the arc of the ball's flight, the bounce, and the second arc of the ball's path between the bounce and the hit.

© Steve Margheim

Andre Agassi sets up behind the ball for a backhand return. He can either step into the shot, or hit from the open stance.

From the turn position move with fast, small steps. Stop on your back, or outside, foot with your toes aligned near the edge of this imaginary flight line. You are now positioned behind the ball. Your body should still be straight up and down from the waist. It should feel as if you were waiting in the turn position for a ball that came directly to you in the first place.

With this precise alignment, you now have the option of stepping in with the front foot, according to the basic model, or hitting off the back foot, doing either from a balanced position. If you are rushed for time, you can hit from this open stance. If not, you can step into the shot with the front foot. When hitting with the traditional closed stance, the step should be toward the target so that a line drawn from your back foot to your front foot would be parallel to the flight of the shot.

Recover

The fourth element in the movement pattern is the recovery. After making the shot, you should recover to the ready position and then shuffle step back toward the center of court. The goal should be to recover to the center of your opponent's two widest possible angles rather than the geometric center of the court. If you are unable to recover fully, you should assume a stationary ready position before your opponent's next hit. This prevents your opponent from hitting behind you when you are still moving. From this stationary ready position, you increase your chances of reaching a ball hit in either direction.

MOVING AT THE NET

The basic sequences for moving to the ball are the same for the volleys and the overhead as they were for the ground strokes. The difference with the volleys is that as you move forward, you must stop and reestablish the ready position before the turn, steps, and ball alignment. You achieve this by using the split step. To spilt step, widen your stance and land on the balls of your feet with your torso straight up and down. Your knees are flexed and you should feel balanced and ready to move in either direction. Whether serving and volleying, or approaching off the ground stroke, you should use the split step to achieve the ready position. Time the split step to begin as your opponent starts the racket forward to the ball. Too many players run through their volleys in an attempt to achieve better net position. As you see your opponent begin to swing, split step into the ready position. You are now on balance and able to follow in any direction the movement patterns presented next.

A critical aspect of moving is staying on balance in all phases of the pattern—in both the movement to the ball and the recovery. This means that you are straight up and down from your waist, with the center of gravity equidistant between your feet. Imagine a line drawn from the top of the head, down the spine, and coming out between the feet. The goal in moving is to keep this imaginary balance line straight and intact.

Court Movement Key Images

The following key images demonstrate how to align behind the flight of the ball with the back foot and hit with an open stance, both on the groundstrokes and the volleys. From this same balanced position behind the ball, the player also has the ability to step into the shot according to the basic stroke models. This flexibility to hit off of either foot is characteristic of a fully developed classical style.

KEY IMAGE 1: FOREHAND ALIGNMENT AND OPEN STANCE

The first photo shows the alignment for moving to the ball on the forehand side. The player has arrived behind the ball on the outside, right foot. The tips of the right toes are positioned along the flight line of the incoming ball. Note the full shoulder turn and complete racket preparation.

The second photo shows that as she executes the hit from this position, her weight will naturally shift forward on the left front foot at contact, with the stance remaining open through the course of the hit. This combination of good shoulder and racket preparation and open stance is common at higher competitive levels.

KEY IMAGE 2: ONE-HANDED BACKHAND ALIGNMENT AND OPEN STANCE

The proper alignment for the one-handed backhand is also with the back foot behind the flight of the incoming ball. One of the most common problems in lower-level tennis is the tendency of one-handed players to reach the ball with a large diagonal cross step. This leads to overrotation, loss of power, and inconsistency. As with the forehand, the outside foot is positioned along the line of the flight of the incoming ball. Note the player is balanced and prepared to hit with a full shoulder and complete racket preparation. From this position, he can step into the line of the shot, or hit from the open position shown in the second photo. His weight will naturally shift to the front foot in the course of the swing, with the angle of the stance unchanged.

KEY IMAGE 3: TWO-HANDED BACKHAND ALIGNMENT AND OPEN STANCE

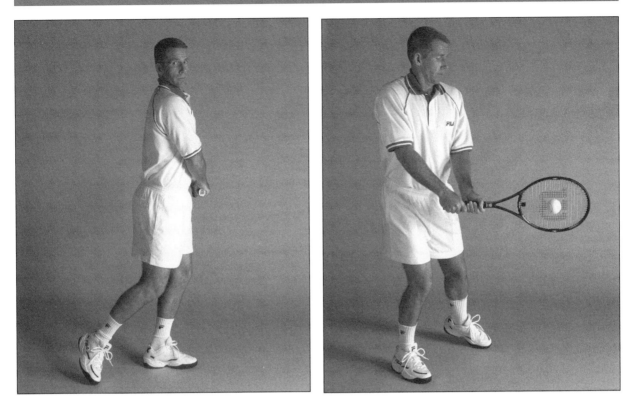

The alignment for the two-handed backhand is a mirror image of the classical forehand. The player reaches the ball with the outside foot and positions it behind the flight of the ball. He now has the option to step into the line of the shot, or execute from the open stance. Note the preparation. He has arrived at the ball and reestablished the turn position with a full shoulder turn, good balance, and full racket preparation. When hitting from the open stance, he will naturally transfer the weight forward to the front foot in the course of the swing, as shown in the second photo.

KEY IMAGE 4: FOREHAND VOLLEY ALIGNMENT AND OPEN STANCE

One of the most difficult aspects of volleying is achieving good alignment and balance in the brief intervals between exchanges in net play. As with the forehand ground stroke, the player should position to the ball with the outside, right foot behind the flight of the ball, as shown in the first photo. Note the complete preparation. The player can now execute the classical volley from a balanced position and maintain the core biomechanical elements, as shown in the second photo. At contact, his weight will naturally shift onto the front foot with the open angle of the stance unchanged.

KEY IMAGE 5: ONE-HANDED BACKHAND ALIGNMENT AND OPEN STANCE

The first photo shows the alignment for moving to the ball on the one-handed backhand volley. As with the ground stroke, it is a mistake to position to the ball with a large cross step. This leads to a loss of balance and a higher degree of shot difficulty. The goal is to reach the ball with the outside, left foot and position along the line of the oncoming ball. The core body and racket preparation is the same. The player can step into the line of the shot, or hit open, as shown in the second photo, with the weight naturally shifting to the front foot in the stance.

KEY IMAGE 6: TWO-HANDED BACKHAND VOLLEY ALIGNMENT AND OPEN STANCE

The basic principle of court alignment is the same whether the player volleys with one hand or two. To achieve good balance, she should reach the ball with the back, left foot. This outside foot is aligned behind the incoming shot, as shown in the first photo. The shoulder turn and racket preparation are complete. The player may then step in, or hit with an open stance, as shown in the second photo. The core biomechanics are unchanged from the basic closed stance, with the weight naturally shifting to the front foot during the hit, shown in the second photo.

CHAPTER 9

PROGRESSIVE STROKE DEVELOPMENT

Once you have worked through the key positions and images for the Visual Tennis stroke models, you can start to build your muscle memory through a special series of progressive exercises and drills. This process is the key to developing strokes that will hold up under pressure. By working progressively through the exercises, you will create strokes that are effortless and pleasurable to hit, and you will eliminate the need for constant analysis and repair.

Exercise 1: Practicing the Model Swing

Build your swing pattern without the ball. Using the four key positions and their corresponding mental images, practice executing the pattern until it becomes smooth and automatic. If possible, do this in front of a full-length mirror. The mirror will help you make sure that you pass correctly through each of the key positions. As an exercise, build up to 5 perfect swings, then 10.

If you are unsure about any point in the pattern, stop and refer to the checkpoints. Refer to the full stroke sequences at the beginning of the particular stroke chapter to improve your feel for the overall motion. You might also study the Visual Tennis video. As you work without the ball, you may find that the model images of the still frames will spontaneously come to mind, guiding the motion. If you are struggling with a particular aspect of the motion, go back and re-create it physically and visually using the checkpoints. Doing these slow, systematic practice swings is particularly vital for beginning players.

Exercise 2: Eyes Closed

Now close your eyes and do the same exercise. Use your mental imagery of the key positions to guide yourself through the motion, beginning with the ready position. Open your eyes at the end of the swing and check the finish position against the checkpoints. Do the same for the turn and the contact. Your ability to replicate the model with your eyes closed is an excellent measure of your mastery of the physical model and the imagery that goes with the key positions. Work until you can do this effortlessly. This will not only improve your muscle memory but also prepare you for the process of keying the strokes using imagery in competitive play.

Exercise 3: Controlled Drill

To develop the ground strokes, volleys, or overhead, you should begin hitting balls in what we call *controlled drill*. This means working with an even feed of slow- to medium-paced balls. A fundamental principle of the Visual Tennis training process is that the work must be progressive. It is impossible to develop or correct a stroke by playing games, or even by rallying. You must have the opportunity to hit a stream of easy, well-placed balls. The balls in controlled drill should come directly to you, without requiring extensive footwork. This low degree of difficulty gives you the freedom you need to begin approximating the model. You can create this controlled feed by working with a practice partner, a teaching pro, or a ball machine. The advantage of the ball machine is the precision of ball placement, which facilitates accurate, consistent execution of the model.

The key to executing the motion is to begin the preparation immediately. This means reacting *when the opponent strikes the ball* and initiating the turn as it comes off your racket. Far too many players do not focus on and react to their opponent's hit. They waste half or more of their limited preparation time waiting until the ball is on their side of the net, or even until it bounces.

Without complete preparation, you will find it impossible to execute the rest of the stroke pattern. The turn should *precede* any movement to the ball, as explained in the previous chapter. On the ground strokes your goal should be to complete the turn as the ball crosses the net to your side. You should be prepared to hit well before the bounce. On the volleys you should strive to complete the turn by the time the ball is halfway to you at the net.

If you are a beginner and find it difficult to execute the turn motion before the ball reaches you, or if you have had problems with your preparation in the past, you should start in the turn position when you begin controlled drill. Move from the ready position to the turn position *before* the ball starts toward you, with your racket and body aligned according to the checkpoints. After you can execute the stroke from the turn position, you can begin in the ready position and develop the full motion.

© Steve Margheim

Pete Sampras keeps his balance by landing on his front foot while kicking away with his back foot.

Work in controlled drill until you can hit 10 strokes according to the model. As you hit balls, you should also do muscle-memory corrections, as explained below. These will allow you to monitor the technical progress of your stroke. When you can hit 10 strokes with precision, increase the speed of the ball feed and the number of repetitions.

For the serve, work in one service box for a dozen balls. Then work in the other box. Start slowly and execute the model precisely. If you have trouble with the racket drop you can start in that position to establish it, similar to starting in the turn position for the groundstrokes.

As you work to establish the serve at various levels, do this drill: Start in the deuce court and hit a first serve. If you miss, hit the second serve in deuce court. Now move to the ad court and repeat. This allows you to practice the serves in combination and gain a sense of your serving percentages on both sides.

Exercise 4: Muscle-Memory Corrections

As you work in controlled drill, you can begin to do muscle-memory corrections. Muscle-memory correction is a powerful process that allows you to eliminate your deviations from the model by moving from your current level of approximation to the exact checkpoints for the model. To do a correction, simply freeze and hold your position at the finish of your stroke, wherever it may be. To make the correction, compare your physical position to the checkpoints for the model finish. Adjust your position from wherever you finished to the model, for example, from an 80 percent approximation to the exact model position.

Now close your eyes and visualize the difference in the two positions and how it would feel to make the changes and more closely approximate the model. Visualize the key checkpoints. Now, with your eyes still closed, execute the swing again according to these adjusted key images. Check your position again at the finish. When working in controlled drill, you can do muscle-memory corrections every 5 to 10 balls.

Exercise 5: Successive Approximation Drills

Although some players seem to absorb the models or a certain key position almost instantaneously, most players gradually conform their strokes to the models over time. The change takes place in increments over many repetitions. With more repetitions, the stroke moves closer to the model elements. This process of gradually moving the stroke toward the model is called *successive approximation*.

Do the following exercise to measure your increments of movement toward the model over time. Working in controlled drill or with the higher difficulty drills described later, estimate your approximation to the model on a given ball. Use a scale of 1 to 100. For example, evaluate how close your turn is to the checkpoints. On a ground stroke, if your shoulders are fully perpendicular to the net with your arm accurately in the hitting position, give yourself 100. Evaluate the degree of deviation and keep track over time as you work closer to the model. Do the same for the finish position. Follow the same process on any stroke. You can have your practice partner or teaching pro do the same and then compare the numbers.

Each time you work, you should gain an increment of approximation, which is reflected in your percentage grade. When you can consistently replicate the stroke with 90 to 95 percent accuracy, you are ready to increase the difficulty of your drill or play. Assigning the grades is an enjoyable and effective method of speeding the development of your stroke, particularly for junior players.

Exercise 6: Court Movement

The next step in controlled drill is to add footwork, or movement to the ball. When the ball does not come directly to you—and it almost never does in match play—your goal is to beat the ball to where it is going and be waiting for it in the correct turn position, as if the ball had initially come to you. The previous chapter explains the patterns of movement and the associated key images. Study it before introducing movement into your stroke development.

As with the basic stroke, develop your footwork working with a ball machine if possible. Start by moving two or three steps to the ball and gradually increase the distance. When your stroke production breaks down and you start to deviate from the model, reduce the movement until your execution returns to the 90 to 95 percent level. Gradually make your movement to the ball wider until you can cover both corners of the court. One characteristic of the top classical players is their ability to hit the forehand off the front or back foot, with either an open or closed stance. The footwork chapter will show you how to develop this flexibility. By learning the basic pattern with the closed stance, however, you will find it easier to master the core biomechanical elements.

Do the same basic movement patterns for your volleys, starting in ready position at the net. As you develop your ability to move side to side at the net, you should simultaneously begin practicing your movement forward, doing approach sequences. Again, do this in a controlled fashion. You can set most ball machines to throw simple approach patterns, for example, one short ball followed by two volleys. Your pro or practice partner can feed you the same pattern. In learning to serve and volley, work with a partner in the same fashion. Hit a serve and follow it in. Rather than face a live return, have your partner or pro feed you a first volley and then a second volley. This will allow you to master the split step, the movement patterns, and the execution of the strokes. Progress from this controlled sequence to live serve and volley points.

Exercise 7: Rally Drills

From controlled feed you should progress to rallies, with either a practice partner or your teaching pro, on both ground strokes and volleys. Again, start with moderate pace and minimal movement to the ball. Focus on the immediate completion of the turn. Hit back and forth at an even rhythm and keep the speed of the exchange constant. As in controlled drill, monitor the stroke by grading your approximations to the model and doing periodic muscle-memory corrections.

Progress to the "forever rally game." Count how many balls you and your partner can exchange with a smooth rhythm and close approximation to the model. Both players can be in the backcourt for ground strokes, or one player can be up and one back for volleys. For the volleys start on one half of the court and keep the rally under control. You can play with both players at the net to work on your touch, reflexes, and technique.

Expand the rally to incorporate movement to the ball. On the ground strokes do accuracy drills, hitting crosscourt or down the line. For the volleys expand the rally to include the entire court so that you take more steps to the ball. The best way to do this at first is by setting a ball machine to deliver a varied pattern of balls.

To practice the volleys, have your pro or partner feed you a short ball at about the service line. Now hit an approach and play out the pattern, volleying against the live returns. For the serve, play "no double-fault" points. For example, if you are working on your second serve and hitting with spin, hit *all* second serves. Stay in the deuce court until you hit a serve in. Rally out the point. Then move to the ad court and repeat.

Exercise 8: Intermediate Competitive Games

Before moving to match play, it is vital to play intermediate competitive games that will test your strokes and your keying process under pressure, but under less pressure than you will face in match or tournament play. We call this an *intermediate competitive situation*. In traditional lessons the player makes an apparent improvement as the pro feeds the student easy balls, sometimes directly from a basket at the net. The player then goes from this low-level, controlled drill directly to a match, and the stroke falls apart. Intermediate competitive games allow you to prepare yourself progressively for match play using the keying process under gradually increasing pressure.

To work on your ground strokes in an intermediate competitive game, play backcourt rally games to 4 or to 7 points. Drop and hit to start. The point doesn't count if either player misses the first hit. For the volleys, change the live-approach drill described earlier into a similar game. Have your partner feed the short ball so that you can hit the approach. Play out the points. The first player to win 7 by a margin of 2 wins. Now add the serve at the start of these games. Let one player serve all the points, and play to 7 or 11 points. You can also play the points in the no double-fault format to take the pressure off the serve and increase your confidence in your serving ability.

At this point you should also be working on your key images as described in the next section. These intermediate games help you discover which keys are the most active for you. You will use those keys to build your personal key image charts.

Exercise 9: Grading Your Keying Process

When you begin to develop your strokes, you should grade your approximations to the models on a scale from 1 to 100, as described above. Now add a similar evaluation tool. In your rallies and transitional competitive games, evaluate your success in keying your strokes using your personal keys, that is, grade your control of the keying process. Again, use a scale from 1 to 100. If you were able to key every ball to a specific image, give yourself a score of 100. As with the approximations of the model, strive to achieve a 90 to 95 percent consistently in visualizing your keys.

You can combine both grading systems in the same drill or game. Ask your playing partner or teaching pro to grade your overall approximation to the model on a certain stroke or strokes on a scale of 1 to 100. Grade yourself on your ability to use the key images on the same scale. This dual evaluation process is a powerful way to learn to execute under pressure and find out what is stopping you from executing in certain situations. When you can perform at 90 percent or higher efficiency on *both* scales, you should be able to achieve consistent results in match play.

When you begin to play matches, evaluate your play at the end of a match on the same dual scale. How well did you execute the models? How well did you execute the keying process? Grade yourself from 1 to 100. Initially you expect the numbers to be lower in match play. Reestablish your ability to execute and key by dropping your level of difficulty down to the more basic rally and intermediate competitive situations. Reestablish your ability both to execute your models and to visualize your keys with 90 to 95 percent effectiveness. Now you are ready to test them again in match play. Working this process repeatedly should bring your level of control and execution in practice and match play closer together until you are able to play your best tennis in competition.

Exercise 10: Developing Your Personal Key Images

The ultimate purpose of the Visual Tennis training process is to develop strokes that will be reliable under pressure. Unforced errors and double faults usually result from a breakdown in basic stroke production. Most players vary the pattern of their swing from one ball to the next. When the stroke deviates too far from the correct swing pattern, it breaks down, producing an error.

A breakdown is particularly likely to occur when a player has the opportunity to hit a winner into the open court, either from the backcourt or at the net. The almost universal tendency is to overhit. At tennis below the highest levels, the so-called easy shots are the ones that players miss most often.

This is in part because of poor fundamentals, but the explanation also crosses over into the realm of the mental game. The opportunity to hit a winner creates an emotional expectation that the player should be able to hit the shot. Because most players lack deep confidence in their strokes, they feel pressure and fear that they will miss. This negative expectation is usually self-fulfilling. You have probably seen this pattern repeated ad infinitum in club matches.

Using the key images, you can learn to break this cycle. In the Visual Tennis system, the images become a source of both technical information, positive emotion and, ultimately, confidence. A stroke key image should have a positive emotional component that creates confidence. Don't just imagine the image— imagine yourself making the shot! Visualizing the key in this way gives you the choice to believe in yourself. This provides a method to block fear and execute the stroke. The result is more good shots under pressure.

A former basketball player who took up tennis seriously in his 40s put it this way: "It's just like shooting a jump shot—when you see the ball go in your mind, more shots actually go in."

The basic building blocks of the model are also the basis for the creation of your system of key images. As you develop each stroke you are simultaneously developing the tools you need to stay positive and execute a high-quality technical stroke on easy balls or on any other pressure shot.

A personal key image is a single visual element of the stroke pattern that you use to activate the entire stroke. In the split second before hitting the shot, you visualize the image of the key. By holding this mental image in mind, you trigger the execution of the whole stroke pattern. The key functions as a mental

Pete Sampras maintains the classical arm position all the way through the finish of his backhand.

blueprint, which the body naturally follows. Top players often report seeing spontaneous positive imagery before making shots. The key images in the Visual Tennis system give you a systematic process for developing this ability to previsualize your shot making.

We present these key images for every stroke in the individual chapters. Determine which of these keys are most useful for your game by intuition, trial and error, or comment from a teaching pro. Theoretically, an image of any part of the stroke could be an effective key. Each of the four key positions is a potential key, as are the individual checkpoints for each of the still frames. Players often interpret these images in their own way, focusing on certain details or emphasizing one part of the picture. To develop your keys, play creatively with your imagery and let it guide you.

By working in controlled drill, you must determine whether a given key consistently activates a given stroke. If it does, the key is an active key. As the oncoming ball approaches, visualize your key image. Hold the picture in your mind's eye. As you swing, make the real racket overlap the image. You will find that the image will function almost as a magnet, attracting the racket to the correct position. As you hit balls, work to make the racket and the image correspond precisely. Try this for 10 to 20 balls. If the stroke pattern improves, then the stroke is active for you. Add it to your stroke key chart. Monitor your progress by grading your approximations on a scale of 1 to 100 and by doing muscle-memory corrections.

You may want to experiment with slight variations on any of the images by focusing on one or more of the checkpoints. Test each variation in the progression just described.

As you develop and refine your keys, you will work them into a personal key image chart, as shown on page 174. You can receive a free pad of key image charts by writing to our tennis school at the address found in the preface of this book. The key image chart has two parts. First, it lists the active key images for each stroke. Second, it lists tendencies and corrective key images.

One important aspect of developing your keys is correlating specific keys with your most frequent errors. The ultimate benefit of the stroke key system is that it teaches you to understand the types of mistakes you make and how to correct them on the court. What are your tendencies? What are the counteracting keys? The good news is that your specific deviations from the model will tend to be consistent over time. When a stroke begins to lose its effectiveness, you can usually identify the cause as a recurring tendency.

The Visual Tennis system allows you to do tendency analysis. List the recurring errors and the counteractive keys you have developed for each of these tendencies. For example, if you discover in your work with the model that your contact is consistently behind your body, you will want to work with the image of the contact point. If you are having difficulty with preparation and your tendency is to feel rushed, work with the key image of the turn on that particular stroke.

For each shot you should identify up to four primary keys. You should also list your tendencies, or patterns of error, and correlate them with specific

VISUAL TENNIS KEY IMAGE CHART

Date: _____

Name: _____

Stroke: _____

Key Images:

1. _____

2. _____

3. _____

4. _____

Tendencies:

Tendency: **Key:**

_____   _____

_____   _____

_____   _____

_____   _____

corrective keys. Review the key image chart for each stroke before going to the court. You can also use the chart for offcourt visualization training. During matches keep the charts in your racket bag. If you are having difficulty keying a particular stroke, you can reestablish the keying process by referring to them during game changes. Update these charts frequently as your work within the system progresses and your key images change and evolve.

One of the greatest challenges players face in playing tennis is staying emotionally positive and focused on the process of executing their strokes. They are often consumed by negative thoughts about their games, about their opponents, or about strategic situations that occur during a match. To escape, their minds often wander during points to topics other than tennis. By training yourself to use imagery in match play you can overcome all these tendencies. As noted, top players often previsualize shots spontaneously. The stroke key system provides you a way to do this imagery systematically. Because it uses images, the keying system is nonverbal. Tennis moves too quickly to think about in words. But imagery can flow through your mind at the speed of play on the court. As a top teaching pro and nationally ranked seniors player once told me, "I've always played my best matches when I just follow the images flowing through my mind."

Exercise 11: Video Feedback

At each stage of your development, you should use video to help monitor your progress. The learning process is visual in fundamental ways. It is no surprise then that the most powerful feedback is often direct visual information. Seeing their stroke pattern often discloses much to players dealing with a problem stroke. As one student put it when he saw video of his strokes for the first time, "I realized I had never seen my game from the outside and that the internal mental image of myself was remarkably different than external reality. It was a revelation."

Video allows you to align your image of the model with your actual physical motion. This will help you clearly understand your particular tendencies. You can do this with a teaching pro or with your home video camera. Video yourself in basic controlled drill, at the intermediate competitive stages, and in match play. Taping your matches is the ultimate way to understanding exactly how your game breaks down under pressure. You can then devise keys to counter the breakdowns.

As part of the process, you can make a personal modeling tape of yourself executing the model swings perfectly. If possible you should edit together sequences of yourself executing strokes with technical accuracy in a variety of situations and even set them to your favorite music.

Exercise 12: Using Music for Rhythm

Many top players believe that music helps them establish and maintain rhythm. John McEnroe, Ivan Lendl, and Chris Evert have reported the benefits of practicing to music and even singing songs to themselves during matches.

At our tennis school we regularly use music on the court with our junior players. They enjoy practice much more and their strokes naturally improve. You can experiment with music on court using a portable stereo or Walkman. Once you find a song or series of songs that meshes with the rhythm of your tennis, try singing to yourself during both practice and match play. You will find the flow of the music meshes beautifully with the flow of key images during play.

Megan, a high school team player, had more mental toughness than almost any other junior player who trained at our school. She sang to herself during matches. I rarely saw her choke or miss an easy ball. She attributed this to the effect of music on her play. An avid rock music fan, Megan changed songs frequently to suit her current passion in music or her mood on a given day. I saw her nervous just once before a match—when she was having difficulty finding a new song among her numerous tapes and CDs.

Exercise 13: Offcourt Visual Training

The Visual Tennis system includes a range of offcourt visual training techniques that will supplement your oncourt work. When you are unable to play—during winter weather, if you are injured, or if work or family duties keep you off the court more than you would like—you can add more offcourt visual training to help maintain your skills and continue the training process.

Doing regular offcourt sessions will speed your ability to develop the models, master the keying process, and prepare to play your best tennis in competition. Develop one offcourt training segment for each session on court. Draw the imagery from your work on the basic model and your personal keys. You should see yourself executing the basic stroke and keying your stroke precisely to your personal images. Imagine smooth basic rallies, placements, and running shots. Visualize accurate crosscourt and down-the-line shots. Now put together shot combinations that you want to hit in actual play.

The sessions should be brief—about five minutes. You can do them by sitting in a comfortable chair and closing your eyes. You might also play music. Some players like to stand up and swing the racket according to the images they are visualizing. Others do visual imaging in their free time during the routine of the day.

Building your offcourt image training rituals is an individual process. Experiment with the possibilities until you find comfortable, enjoyable routines. Vary them often to keep them fresh. Zoom in on a particular key. See the strokes in regular time and in slow motion. Focus on how the stroke feels in particular parts of your body, such as the shoulders, the hitting arm, and so on. If you see yourself from the player's perspective, try visualizing yourself from the position of an outside observer, or vice versa. Never do offcourt imaging when you are bored or unmotivated. To be effective it should be fun, and you should be eager!

You can also do your offcourt training by watching video of technically superior strokes. Video can a powerful source of positive technical imagery as well as an emotional inspiration. The Visual Tennis video presents the stroke models using the same progressions as the book. It includes built-in segments that allow you to visualize the key building blocks and the execution of each stroke set to music. Other good sources are the Sybervision tapes with Stan Smith and Chris Evert, and *The Winning Edge*. Tape matches with Pete Sampras or other players who hit the stroke with the classical style. If you can make a personal modeling tape, as described earlier, use it as a regular part of prematch preparation. At our tennis schools we often set these tapes to the favorite music of our junior players, who use them for prematch preparation.

Watch tennis matches on television or in person. Seek out players with technical elements of the classical models you are developing. As you watch them imagine yourself on the court executing the same shots. Many players have the experience of playing far above their normal level after intently observing top players. You can make this experience a regular part of your tennis training.

Visualization is also one of the most powerful elements for prematch preparation. Do five minutes of visual imaging in the car on the way to the match (but don't close your eyes if you're driving). Watch five minutes of video before going to the court. Or do both. Use your instincts and imagination to construct the sequences and exact images you feel you will need to execute and play your best in a specific match.